Premium Is the New Black

Alan O'Neill has completed some inspirational work for us at Dalata Hotel Group plc over the past number of years. His insight into customer experience and customer thought process is second to none. The timing of this book is excellent, as the world of digital collides with traditional hospitality and customer service more frequently.

Those of us in the business of selling will find this book provides us with the wisdom and tools to increase sales.

Stephen McNally, Deputy Chief Executive, Dalata Hotel Group plc

In his unique and compelling manner, Alan O'Neill brings alive one of today's most provocative subjects for contemporary business leaders.

With retail in its most dire state in living memory and the unrelenting charge of the disruptors seeming to have many of the high streets stalwarts on their knees, many have at long last started to realise that this fierce battle for the customer might well mean the death of many of the losers.

Alan convinces all businesses that they are as 'unique as their fingerprints', but treat their customers just like everyone else. Anyone can copy your strategy but no one can copy your culture – its high time you mobilised and energised these points of difference through the customer experience.

Premium is the New Black is a must read for anyone battling for the customers attention and ongoing loyalty.

Rene Carayol MBE, International Keynote Speaker,
Author and Leadership Guru, Author of Spike

If we had any doubts about how banks are providing a commodity to their markets, the changes taking place particularly in the UK make it very clear. Supply has to be kept steady and consistent – taken for granted – and service has to improve. The Competition and Markets Authority is driving change through Open Banking that will digitise so much delivery and allow consumers to make decisions based on full and consistent transparency.

This will encompass not just pricing and product types for comparison, but also service levels and Trip Advisor style reviews. It'll be a fusion of technology that won't allow the provider to achieve success without a business model that genuinely delivers great service in parallel. The pressure is on!

We've worked with Alan many times across the years and engaged on several subjects, but his passion for customer experience is always apparent – he gets it. He knows what customers and businesses expect, as well as being able to stand

at the side and point out the routes for success. His insight has never been so relevant as it is today, and tomorrow!

Steven Cochran, Head of Products & Growth Platforms, Allied Irish Bank GB

The retail landscape has become a battle-ground for customer loyalty. The recent cycle of heavy promotional activity to drive footfall is unsustainable, and businesses have to adapt to become a truly customer-led organisation to survive.

At Ann Summers, I have worked with Alan over a number of years, and highly value his expertise in creating a future-facing retail business that moves us from a transactional, profit driven model to a purpose-driven brand, inspired and led by our customers. Alan helped us to see that we need to surprise and delight our customers, to attract new customers to our brand based on great product and experiences whether they shop with us in store, online or at a party.

I know that Alan's take on this new generation of retail, will be immensely valuable in helping organisations to grow their businesses in the future.

Jacqueline Gold CBE, CEO, Ann Summers

For too long now, 'customer service' initiatives have been rolled out with the objective of reducing costs rather than improving service. Customers tell us they're at their wits' end, with two out every three left feeling exhausted when dealing with customer care. But from this unhappiness however, comes opportunity. Organisations that embrace their customers, that truly put them first, will be rewarded with increased sales and sustained loyalty.

BT have worked with Alan O'Neill, not just to help with our own customer service, but to educate our customers on how they can help their customers. You can't ask for any more than Alan's track record of success. His insights garnished from customer service case studies across all industries make him a front runner in his field.

Joe Walsh, Head of Unified Communications, BT Telecom

In this incredibly fast paced world it's often hard to keep up with change and yet Alan keeps things simple, easy to understand and inevitably 'hits the nail on the head.' His knowledge of what's right for business comes from years of experience working with the worlds best companies; asking the right things of the right people... in other words those closest to your customer.

Duncan Graham, Director of Retail (Ireland, Scotland and Spain), Specsavers

Change Management and Customer Experience are two very relevant topics in today's world. Every single client of ours is going through change at some level - some more disruptive than others. Within that change, more and more organisations have come to realize that whatever change they make, they must put 'customer' at the heart of that.

'Customer Experience' is indeed the new battleground and differentiator in this digital world. As a highly experienced Change Agent and Speaker, Alan inspires and challenges audiences with his practical business models and stories. The Selfridges Story is just one that brings all of the concepts to life and resonates with busineses of all types, B2B and B2C.

Cosimo Turroturro, Managing Director, Speaker's Associates

We can all agree that an exceptional customer experience is a powerful engine for long term growth and success. But how to do it?...that's the challenge!

Alan helped me by sharing years of experience with many diverse businesses. His insights are powerful but more importantly he tackles the question with a degree of imagination and enthusiasm that is inspiring. This book is a 'keeper' for anybody who is truly focused on the long term success of their business.

Donal Forde, Ex Managing Director, AIB Bank (RoI)

In order to be succesful in today's business landscape you have to build a winning culture. It is all about being a customer champion and taking ownership.

When working with Alan in deBijenkorf, I found him to a great catalyst for this change while asking the hard questions and driving productive discussions.

Edo Beukema, Member of the Management Board and
Chief Merchandise Officer, HBC Europe - Galeria Kaufhof GmbH

The majority of businesses spend most of their time and budgets on acquiring new customers and developing new product. However what happens before and after the customer is acquired? This should be the organisation's North Star!

I have worked with Alan on a number of projects over the years, and his number one focus is 'the customer', specifically, how to delight them. Alan has worked with some great iconic brands helping them to focus on delighting customers - while others lost their way by focusing on the latest trend. This often results in them losing their customers. Alan truly believes 'Premium is the new Black' and has proven this over and over again.

This book will be a great read, filled with practical and brilliant examples and tips.
Lorraine Sweeney, Senior Partner, Ceres Energy

Alan is one of the most brilliant minds in department store retailing today. Before engaging him for Rustan's for a short-term project, I heard nothing but good things on the work he did for Selfridges. Having met him in Rome in 2015, I was impressed by the breadth and depth of his knowledge on two critical areas: company culture and the customer experience.

I have learned from Alan, that even in this digital era the secret sauce of an organization is people – and stretching it further, relationships. The quality of the experience we deliver, and resilience in this turbulent age is 100% dependent on the quality of our RELATIONSHIPs.

Alan said it simplifies to two things that need to be holistically and deeply understood and harnessed not only functionally but also creatively: TALENT and TECHNOLOGY. Alan has this rare skill of helping businesses like ours continue to focus on our very basic purpose of firstly winning loyalty of our employees and then our customers. It's still about sincerely and authentically winning and retaining hearts and minds; even in this age of big data, crypto currency, block chain, and other game changing disruptions.

Alan has useful insights on how to disrupt yourself but in a way that has clarity, that is still true to your dna, and at the end of the day is still about people. Alan completed a project for us where we picked his brains and connected with his wisdom and passion. That was fascinating and enlightening. I can't wait to read this book.
Donnie Tantoco, President, Rustan Commercial Corporation, Philippines

My partner and I started a new business, where 'service' of course is the key differentiator. SwimGym.com. It's a menber's only swimming pool and coaches have olympic or international competition background. So, thank you Alan for all your good coaching when we worked together in deBijenkorf in Netherlands.
Robert Bohemen, Chief Marketing Officer / SVP Global Marketing, TomTom

I am proud to say that I have witnessed Alan delivering outstanding seminars, presentations and small group development sessions and rarely have I experienced such a captivating leader and presenter. He has the unique talent of holding his audience in the palm of his hand and his extensive retail knowledge and experience is second to none.

In my 35 years retail experience Alan is top of the league. I was also very fortunate to be mentored by him for sometime. A fantastic experience. If he offers this to you then you only need two words. Yes please!

Peter Larkin, Senior Operations Manager, Alshaya – Egypt

In my 20+ years' experience placing some of the world's greatest speakers with client companies, the subject of Customer Experience has never before been so prevalent. With all of the changes that digital brings, it's the traditional approach to customer experience that has become more relevant than ever. But some elements of the traditional have also changed and in this book, Alan walks us through an interesting and practical approach that will suit any business.

There is no doubt in my mind that 'customer experience is the new battleground' and that should be a mantra for every organisation, B2C or B2B.

Brendan O'Connor, Founder, Castle Management, UK.

EIQA has developed a 'Service – Performance' model that forms the backbone of our Quality Management Systems (QMS) assessment methodology. We are honoured to have Alan on the panel of judges for The National Q Mark Awards. Alan is in the unique position of not only understanding this model, he really believes in it too. He can clearly demonstrate that there is a link between engaged employees and why they should be at the very heart of an effective customer service strategy.

Irene Collins, Managing Director, Excellence Ireland Quality Association

Alan O'Neill has been an inspiration, not only in business advice through articles that he has written in the Sunday Independent, but also as a non-executive director to our not-for-profit charity (County Kildare Local Employment Service) based throughout Co. Kildare.

We are a publicly funded Public Employment Service, and with the constant backing of Alan's motivational, positive influence and endless energy, we have succeeded in meeting (and beating) targets, under-budget, and on time! His charismatic manner and powerfully upbeat drive, has opened doors for us that previously remained firmly shut! We thank him for his keen interest in our clients, our partners and in Corporate Social Responsibility... and for keeping our 'full employment' dream alive.

Clodagh Judge, Chief Operations Officer,
County Kildare Local Employment Service

Customer Experience has always been an important topic for all businesses in Lebanon. Lebanese organisations are changing mindsets and 'thinking customer' much more than ever.

We at ESA Business School are leading the way for businesses in our region and are happy to have Alan support us on that journey.

Michèle El Khoury, Programme Manager,
École Supérieure des Affaires (ESA) Executive Education – Beirut

Change and disruption are the new norms in business today. More and more of our clients are coping with that by staying focused on their customer. Customers are changing too and their expectations continue to grow. That applies to digital and traditional channels.

Alan's book brings us back to basics and challenges us all to refresh our thinking, putting customer experience at the heart of our decision-making.

We have worked with Alan countless times as a speaker and our clients continue to be inspired by his practical tips and stories.

Nick Gold, Managing Director, Speakers Corner

Alan's business acumen, genuine passion for great customer service and his hands-on experience overseeing large-scale change within organisations such as Selfridges is unique. It makes him one of the most impressive Change Management and Customer Experience consultants I have come across. Alan is a popular speaker at events around the globe with organisations who want to learn from his insights and his bold tactics to help build a world-class customer-centric culture and ultimately to increase sales.

Frances Keane, CEO – Personally Speaking

Premium Is the New Black

In a world of dynamic change, put *Customer Experience* at the heart of your decision-making

Alan O'Neill

The Change Agent

alanoneill.biz

ORPEN PRESS

Published by
Orpen Press
Upper Floor, Unit K9
Greenogue Business Park
Rathcoole
Co. Dublin
Ireland

email: info@orpenpress.com
www.orpenpress.com

Paperback ISBN: 978-1-78605-066-3
ePub ISBN: 978-1-78605-067-0

A catalogue record for this book is available from the British Library.

Printed in Dublin by SPRINTprint Ltd

ABOUT THE AUTHOR

With over 30 years of experience from the board room to the front line, ***Alan O'Neill*** *MBA, The Change Agent* has supported iconic brands to achieve amazing results. In a dynamic world, he knows what it takes to drive *change* in a business, from top to bottom and back to front. It's about having a *Customer Centric Culture, Engaged People,* and a *Supercharged Sales Effort.*

One sector in particular that has probably seen more disruption than any other is retail. Alan was the lead consultant that navigated Selfridges through significant change from 'bricks only' to 'clicks and bricks'. Up to 2004, Selfridges was a sleeping giant, but it's now officially the *Best Department Store in the World,* and one of the most profitable (per m^2).

Alan has been privileged to support many iconic brands to achieve success. But it's not just about retail. Across B2B, B2C and the public sector, his clients include global brands like AIB Bank, Harrods, Eli Lilly, Intel, Lufthansa, Mercedes, Moet Hennessy, Ramada Hotels, Scottish Power, Sherry Fitz, St. Gobain, The UN, Vodafone and more.

He is a consultant, trainer, and non-exec director, and a visiting professor with ESA Beirut. He is also a trusted mentor to many C-Level executives that seek his support. Alan has a reputation for making the complex simple, and being down-to-earth and practical, with a commercial focus that brings everything back to the customer. Alan now writes a weekly business advice column for the *Sunday Independent,* Ireland's leading business newspaper. He is a contributor to other publications such as the *Daily Telegraph.*

It is this unrivalled business acumen that has seen Alan chair and speak at conferences around the world and conduct masterclasses with C-Level executives. He asks hard and uncomfortable questions to inspire and provoke actions: *Should you refresh your culture to prepare for emerging global challenges? How will you overcome cynicism and resistance to change? How do you overcome complacency and lack of accountability? How will you differentiate with a customer-experience culture? How do you retain the best talent? How do you increase sales in a challenging and disruptive global market?*

Alan O'Neill | *The Change Agent*
Consultant | Speaker | Non-exec Director | Columnist

For enquiries about speaking engagements or masterclasses, go to www.alanoneill.biz

Alan's company is Kara Change Management
www.kara.ie

ACKNOWLEDGEMENTS

My thanks to family, friends, all in KARA, strategic partners and associates. Your ongoing support and inspiration is invaluable. You are a constant source for fresh and objective ideas.

A particular mention goes to all the clients that I have personally worked with since 1991. It is a privelege to have the opportunity to support and challenge you when you need it. But in truth, as a 'corporate anthropologist', I have learned more from you than I have from any academic book. You may recognise that I have adapted here the best of what makes you the greatest in your field.

I will be forever indebted to five great business mentors that I was fortunate to work with over the last forty years. RON SEDGWICK is my pseudonym for you.

As it is my debut book, I had a lot to learn. In making it a finished product, I want to thank Peter O'Connell, a great literary agent and publicist. I also wish to thank Gerry Kelly and all at Orpen Press.

A final word of thanks to you the reader, for taking the time to make change a priority and put customer at the heart of your business.

Alan O'Neill.

CONTENTS

Welcome from the Author

As the volume, speed, and complexity of change accelerates exponentially, businesses around the world and across industry are trying to cope in a new marketplace. But where is all this change coming from? The four main drivers of change – sociological, political, economic, and technological – illustrate it.

Sociologically, people are different in terms of behaviours and attitudes. For example, there is a strong health and wellness agenda where people are more educated about what is good for them. People are more informed and have a stronger social and environmental conscience. Millennials in particular are concerned about provenance and trust their friends and social media review sites more than traditional advertising. Let's not forget about what it's like for a toddler growing up in this new world of swiping up, down, left, and right!

The economy is changing dramatically as we speak. Currency fluctuations, interest rates, and some countries and regions are in growth, while others are in decline. Minimum wage rates and insurance costs are going up, causing some small businesses in particular to downsize and owners of SMEs to work more hours themselves.

The political landscape is changing. At a macro level, geographic borders in some parts of the world are under threat. Demographic governments are constantly making promises to their electorates based on short term goals in order to get re-elected. Legislation and compliance is a growing phenomenon, as can be seen with data protection, for example. Consequently, banks and other companies are having to build up resources significantly to cope with the extra demands placed on them to be squeaky clean.

Let's not forget about technology and the massive effect it is having on the world. Moore (one of the founders of Intel in the 60s) predicted back then that the capacity of a chip would double every two years. That just means that for example, the processors, mainframes, and memory banks that would have required the space of a football stadium then can now fit on your desk, or indeed in the cloud! The growth in digital and mobile is phenomenal. Technology is the single biggest driver of change and probably has the most effect of all four drivers.

In reality, all four drivers of change are intertwined and sometimes interdependent. You can't say exclusively that one causes the other, but what you can acknowledge is the business impact. Some key trends have emerged as a result of the collision of all four drivers. Globalisation is an example where trade barriers and import tariffs have fallen. A customer in Co. Kerry in Ireland can now buy a handbag from a retailer in the U.S. A consultant sitting at home in Toronto can provide solid consultancy advice on-line to a client in Singapore. An executive compelled to achieve income after redundancy can set up shop in his home kitchen and sell product to anywhere in the world.

Another trend is commoditisation. More and more service providers are coming to terms with the reality that they cannot differentiate on product alone. As technology improves, the barriers to entry for new competitors reduce. It's getting easier to copy established brands quite quickly. Banks recognise this. Where in the past they might have thought they could differentiate their mortgage products, they now realise that is not the case. A mortgage is a mortgage is a mortgage, regardless of where you get it. Of course, there might be some subtle differences, but over its lifetime of 20-30 years, it's usually not that much.

How then can organisations differentiate? This book argues that the next great battleground is not in product differentiation, but in customer experience. That, of course, means different things to different people in varying industries. The book breaks that out in structured detail. Much of that customer experience is still face to face.

Here, I draw concepts from iconic global brands across many industries that are No1 in their respective areas. I will show how you can apply great customer experience strategies to *your* business, regardless of what industry you're in or what size you are.

Going back to the market stalls of Biblical times, retailing, for example, is one of the oldest commercial industries. Retailers have become very sophisticated since then, and yet, it's the basic things that retailers do very well day-in and day-out that drive sales. If your business interactes with customers, and if your business has a need for sales, you probably have much more in common with retailers than you think.

Retailers move at pace, are very commercial, and are in touch with customers face-to-face every single day. They are an excellent barometer for what's happening on the ground and are usually the first to feel a turn in the economy – good or bad. Retailers can also react very quickly by changing a display, repositioning a slow seller to prime space, dressing a mannequin, or whatever it takes to drive sales fast. Tailored accordingly, these disciplines can work for your business too.

Not only that, but of all industries, retail is the one that seems to have been affected the most by change in recent years. From single channel retailing (face-to-face over the counter) to multiple channel (ordering by telephone, by post or on-line) to omni-channel (a hybrid of all of the above but much more complex), retailers have been at the forefront of all that is good and challenging in business. Undoubtedly the lessons that retailers have learned can be applied to all businesses, regardless of industry. Remember, too, that despite all the technology developments and the digital revolution, the vast majority of retail sales are done in store. Customer experience driven by human interactions is still the primary measure of excellence.

But it's not just about retail! It's just that *everybody* relates to and knows something about retail, as we all shop at some time or another. Indeed, the models and concepts in this workbook have been tested with great success in other industries such as:

- Construction
- Energy financial services/banking
- FMCG, distribution and sales
- FMCG, manufacturing and sales
- Hospitality
- Industrial
- Manufacturers and distributors – various motor industry
- Medical and clinical, optical, dental etc.
- Professional services, such as accountants, auctioneers, brokers, solicitors, consultants
- Retail, large multiples
- Retail, small and independent
- Semi-state
- Service industry
- Tourism
- Transport
- Travel

In other words, the concepts will work in any industry that has customers, business to consumer (B2C) and business to business (B2B).

Let's not forget about the public sector, where government or international agencies are providing a service that is funded by taxpayers. There is a growing trend around the world where such agencies are now prioritising customer service as a key objective. I've seen it first-hand as I have a number of agencies as clients across Europe.

This book focuses on how to build a customer centric culture, where great customer service should be the default business operating model for your organisation, whether you're B2C, B2B, or public sector. The focus is mainly on traditional interactions with your customers – it is not intended to be a book on how to maximise your digital customer experiences. Ultimately the concepts presented here will give you sound, practical tips to drive more sales across all of your customer touchpoints. The ideas are taken from working with some of the best blue-chip global brands and distilled into a format that you can use today.

A fundamental principle at the heart of this book is that when customers have a great experience, they are more likely to buy from you today and tomorrow and be strong advocates for your brand. The book is designed as a practical common-sense tool to help you make sense of the subject. Using your own gut instinct, you just need to apply the ideas and the experiences expressed here to your own business. In reality, all the concepts are tried and tested already and have worked for businesses of all sizes right across industry.

This is not intended to be a scientific or academic book. There are lots of other books in that genre. Rather, it pulls all the concepts together in a practical way and will give you the tools and the opportunity to initially look in at your business in a structured fashion. It will then challenge you to take action and make sound improvements. Your sales will grow if you do nothing else. But if you then go on to use the models to drive more footfall in your business, practice the secrets to convert more prospects and browsers and engage with the tactics to increase their average spend, your sales will grow beyond your expectations.

Every month, there seems to be a new chef appearing on the scene, with great new recipes to whet your appetite and to challenge you. But there are not many new ingredients out there! Likewise, I acknowledge that many of the concepts and ideas presented here are in the public domain already. But over the years, while working with some amazing clients, I have been absorbing the best of what makes them great. In this book is my 'recipe', using the tastiest and most practical ingredients that I have come across.

Good luck.
Alan O'Neill

Part One

Why Is Premium Customer Experience So Essential?

Chapter One

The Business Case for Great Customer Experience

It's always good practice to take time out to look at your business. Whether the economy is up or down should not matter. The reality, however, is that most managers are so busy doing the day job that they don't get time to lift their heads and check their direction. The risk is that the business may be tracking in a way that is not in line with original intentions.

Let's remind ourselves that every commercial organisation would like to have more of some or all of these:

- Market share
- Sales
- Profit
- Satisfied long-term customers
- Customer advocacy
- Relevance
- Brand alignment and reputation
- Great leaders and managers
- Productive people

Even 'not-for-profit' organisations like to have:

- An effective business operating model that ensures that business objectives are delivered efficiently, effectively and within budget
- Productive people and a sense of pride working in their organisation
- Great customer feedback

As the focus on customer experience grows and as customers' expectations increase, great customer experience has become a basic requirement these days for commercial and non-profit organisations.

Customer experience is one of those terms that businesses use loosely and regularly, in business-to-business (B2B) industries such as manufacturers, distributors, etc., in business-to-consumer (B2C) industries such as hotels, retailers, and so on. It's also common language that's used regularly by customers themselves. Of course, everyone assumes they know what it means, and no doubt they do – but you'll see in the next chapter that it can mean very different things to many different people. This is all the more reason to take time and understand what it means specifically for you.

Let's start with the customer. Often, when customers complain, their issues are just dropped into the metaphorical 'basket' of *customer service* and *customer complaints*. How many times have you witnessed a friend telling a story at a dinner party, where they relate a tale of woe or a shoddy experience they've recently had? It might have been a failed promise, a late delivery, a rude salesperson, or whatever. Once they've made their point and wound themselves up again in the re-telling of the story, someone will take out that 'basket', pop the issue in there with a sweeping summary comment and say, 'That's terrible service!' Of course, they're right.

It shouldn't be difficult, but the risk here is that the 'basket' can get needlessly complicated. Far too often within organisations, that 'basket' expands and expands, and the real issues are not dealt with effectively by the organisation for the long term. In larger organisations, too often the basket gets passed unfairly to the Customer Service Manager for fixing, when really the issues are operational in effect and caused by culture in the first place. Think cause and effect here.

If this sounds familiar to you and that is what happens in your organisation – and you want to address it – maybe it's time to think differently.

Literally thousands of books have been written on this subject over the years. Every month, a new guru comes along and presents ideas on service in a new and often very interesting way. In fact, at the time of writing, Google reports 1.2b results to the *customer service* prompt, so it's a popular subject indeed. Customer service is not rocket science and there are some key principles that we'll outline here to show how you *can* achieve great service in a simple way. Keep in mind the power of simplicity.

Where it all began

The concept of customer service is as old as commerce itself. From the beginning of time, traders bartered their wares in return for something of equal or greater value: spices for salt, gold for weapons, liquor for peace, etc. In markets of ancient times, traders sold their products for money. That money made it possible for them to have a standard of living, pay their staff and other expenses and re-invest in more products to sell. And so commerce began.

In today's highly competitive and globalised world, there are few situations where a seller has a monopoly in their market. In such situations, buyers have no choice but to buy from that single source, regardless of how they are treated. Even if the seller is rude, slow, inefficient, arrogant, or poorly presented, buyers will still reluctantly buy if they need or want the product on offer.

Let's deal with this now and get it out of the way. If you are lucky enough to have a monopoly and be the only seller in your industry of a must-have product with no competition, perhaps *customer experience* is not quite as critical for you. As long as your customers *must* have your product, you can do what you like and treat them however you like. The point being made here is not at all intended to promote poor service, but to illustrate that you just might get away with it.

Think for a moment, however; how do your customers feel about buying from you if you are the only game in town? Is it a pleasant, enjoyable and easy experience for them? Will you be able to dominate your market forever and always be the only game in town? Do you and your team even value or actually enjoy giving great service? Will competition ever arrive? Because if and when it does, the chances are that your customers will defect and will probably delight in doing so.

If like the majority of businesses, you do have competition, then your customers have choices regarding who they might buy from. So why will a customer choose one provider over the other? There are practical reasons and emotional reasons which customers will work out for themselves and act on accordingly. Your challenge as an organisation is to plan your points of differentiation proactively and use that to gain custom.

The criteria that help customers decide and differentiate are well documented, and while price is often in the top five, it is seldom top of that list.

Where does price fit into the differentiation debate?

Why do we as customers buy from one seller over another? Is it just to do with price? A common but mistaken view is that customers are motivated mainly by the lowest price. If so, then why do quality brands like Selfridges, Disney, Four Seasons, Chanel, and Louis Vuitton still exist and experience growth? Each one is known for many great attributes, but not for the lowest prices. Similarly, why do premium airlines like Emirates, British Airways, Lufthansa and Aer Lingus still exist? Why doesn't everybody in Europe fly Ryanair, who claim to have the cheapest fares? And in recent years, why are Ryanair even trying to become more customer focused and cuddly? It's because they know that they can get better prices and a different customer segment, as with the frequent business traveller.

Of course price is important. Nobody wants to be ripped off, especially when money is tight. Equally, there are many shoppers who shop in discount retailers like Wal-Mart and Aldi because they like their low prices, and that is their top priority. But thankfully for other non-discount retailers, it's a lower (yet significant) percentage of the consumer market. There are many other drivers such as quality of product, exclusivity, newness, brand loyalty, courtesy, friendliness, advice, information, access, and ambience, that influence a buyer. In this edited list, sellers will of course find opportunities to differentiate and make themselves attractive to consumers.

To allow yourself to fall into the 'low-price' segment of the market is like classifying what you do and your product/service as a mere commodity.

Look at the world of travel retail (duty free shops) who have effectively driven a discount message over the years. There was a time when discounting was their main point of differentiation. But they are learning very fast as they come to terms with changes in their industry. The laws for duty/tax-free purchases continue to change. In Europe in particular, duty and tax-free purchases are not allowed for EU members travelling within the EU. Furthermore, while it's currently a hugely profitable department, lawmakers are also looking closely at alcohol and tobacco sales in the world of duty free from an ethical point of view. That can only be even more challenging to the discount message in the long term.

The difference in price between travel retail and downtown is and will be marginal going forward (if there is even a difference at all). What will travel retail shops do then? Another challenge they face is that some of the airlines – who are directly competing with the airport for retail sales – strongly encourage and scare passengers by telling them to go to the boarding gate as soon as possible. That means that customers have less time in the terminal for shopping.

That industry needs to find additional factors to help their shops differentiate from each other and from the high street – beyond price. Conveniences such as home-delivery, shop-and-collect, pack sizes, impulse gift purchasing and customer experience might be big opportunities and drivers in their future. Personal, fast service, from friendly salespeople to passengers in a hurry, has to help too.

To position and add further context to why service is so important, check out the great book *The Experience Economy*. The authors, B. Joseph Pine II and James H. Gilmore, tell the story of the simple life of a coffee bean to illustrate a great point about price versus customer experience. Here it is:

> Coffee beans are harvested and then sold on the commodity market, just like wheat, gold, silver, oil, etc. *Commodities* in general are sold mainly on price with very tight margin. Let's call that Level 1. But when the coffee beans make their way to Lavazza in Turin (for example) to be roasted, blended and ground, Lavazza then sell their finished coffee as a *product*, at a higher price than when as a bean. Lavazza's expertise, differentiation and USP (unique selling proposition) in blending is rewarded. Call that Level 2.
>
> At Level 3, ground coffee is purchased by coffee shops, where a barista adds further value and differentiation by making a gorgeous espresso, americano, cappuccino or whatever your favourite coffee type is. You might happily queue for this and pay for the *service* you are getting, which will include milk, sugar, napkins, seating, air conditioning and other facilities. In return for the effort and service you'll pay more than the mere cost of the coffee beans, or indeed the cost of pack of coffee on the supermarket shelf.
>
> But what if you go to a Four Seasons Hotel, where you will most likely have a coffee in plush surroundings, with great ambience and space, cushioned armchair seats, table service with no queues, linen napkins, silver cutlery and

attentive waiters? With that amazing experience, your perception will be one of further added value. You will of course expect to pay an added premium for that experience and be happy to do so. This is Level 4.

The four stages or levels are *commodity, product, service* and *experience.*

Differentiation				
High				Four Seasons L4 **Experience**
			Coffee Shop L3 ***Service***	
		Ground Coffee L2 ***Product***		
Low	Beans L1 ***Commodity***			
	Low	***Price***		Premium

If it takes 40-50 coffee beans to make a cup of coffee, see how the price changes along the way, from *commodity* level to *experience*, depending on the extent of differentiation and added value.

Why does nobody ever complain about the price of a coffee in Starbucks? It's because of the perceived value that they are getting versus making it themselves. Likewise, the difference in the price of a coffee in a five-star hotel (compared to Starbucks) is clearly justified. Customers going to Four Seasons know that they will pay more than twice the price of a high street coffee, and yet, they won't even blink an eye.

So where do you see your product/service... as a *commodity, product, service* or *experience*? More importantly, how do you communicate that to your customers and to your own people? While there are very successful businesses in the coffee industry at every level, from commodity stage (L1) to premium experience stage (L4), you have to make a decision for your business. Here you have a choice. Where do you *want* to be? How do you want to differentiate? Once you decide and build your business on that model, pricing and customers' expectations need to merge. Customer service is still important for each level. It's just that the level of experience needs to be relative.

Just as a thought and as an example:

There are very successful organisations operating at each level described above. But service is important to each one, relative to its market. If you decide to build your model on giving great customer *experiences* (top level), you then need to decide how to charge for it. Analysis of market forces, trends and competition will help you decide on the right answer.

In a nutshell, you will get higher prices for your product or service – provided you show clear differentiation and added value compared to a lower priced alternative.

Differentiation

Differentiating your business and product/service from the competition is critical in business. In the first half of the 20th century, when new and previously undreamed-of products were being developed, such as washing powder, washing machines, and TVs, organisations could differentiate on product alone. In the second half of the century, as competition increased, differentiation tended to be achieved through marketing. We're now living in an age where customers are more in control than ever, and they expect more. Excellence in supply chain management is now a new opportunity for differentiation.

Some innovative technology companies, such as Apple, still differentiate with product. But the speed at which competitors can copy and indeed improve upon the original is amazing. As soon as the iPad was launched, competitors such as Samsung, Dell, HP, and Google pushed versions of their respective tablet devices. Apple fans will argue that the other competitor tablets are not a patch on the iPad. Maybe they're right, but you can't blame Samsung and others for taking on Apple. They can't just stand back and let their main competitor have a market to itself. As it happens, Samsung too has fans, and those fans expect innovation from Samsung.

Bear in mind that product imitation is less difficult now, with the cost of entry for many industries coming down. Technology plays a big part in that, and it applies pretty much across the board. It doesn't take so long to bring thoughts and inventions to life.

> *In the past we have always worked on the basis that quality and style will differentiate a product from our customers and thus bring extra sales. These days it is not enough to maintain sales, never mind for getting growth.*
>
> *The consumer is spoilt with choice; so, what can we do to reach their spending? Good service is not enough, it has to be outstanding service. If a consumer ticks a box saying your company is 'satisfactory', this will not cut the mustard in this changing and demanding world.*
>
> *In Alan O'Neill's book 'Premium is the New Black', you will find the answers to manage the growing expectations of consumers, trade buyers, in fact, all purchasing from B2B to B2C!*
>
> Patrick Gardner, Owner and Managing Director, T&G Woodware UK

Can you differentiate on product alone?

In addition to product, retailers in particular need to focus on other elements of the retail mix for differentiation. If it's accepted that most brands can be purchased in several outlets, why should a customer buy from one retailer over the other? Convenience and access might sometimes be a factor, but if all things are equal, something else has to kick in.

For example, a 16cm Le Creuset saucepan can be purchased in any number of retailers on Oxford Street in London. In a recent check, it was the exact same price in each one. Some customers will buy it in John Lewis because they are regular customers of that store. Others will want to buy it in Selfridges. That may be to get the yellow bag and gift wrapping... it may be to get one-to-one personal attention and advice... it may be due to access... or it may just be that Selfridges recognise that they need to differentiate and make the shopping experience a more enjoyable one than other retailers. Every organisation needs to work out what its point of difference can and should be.

In non-food retail, commercial buyers are expected to visit the four corners of the world, edit what they see and bring back portfolios to suit their own corporate store brand and their stores. In their travels, buyers try to negotiate for exclusive product, or at least exclusive product launches. In a world where brands are very powerful, such as Louis Vuitton, Prada, Gucci or Chanel, exclusivity is more and more difficult to achieve for the department store. These strong global brands have great control of their own market. Many of them have their own stand-alone stores and often prefer to operate as concessions within department stores. This changes the dynamic and shifts the power somewhat. They control and decide what stores they'll partner with. Exclusivity in this case is usually decided by the brand and not by the retailer.

Some buyers crack this challenge with 'own-label', where they try to differentiate by using their own company name as the brand, such as Marks & Spencer, Next, Tesco Milk, etc. This works best where high volume is possible in order to gain advantage from the economies of scale. That doesn't mean that own-label is the only key to differentiation. If that was the case, why wouldn't Tesco remove all non-Tesco branded products and do everything in own-label? Does it also mean that Marks & Spencer only have to concern themselves with product? Of course not – customers are motivated by a combination of drivers, seldom by one alone.

Whichever way you look at it or try to rationalise it, differentiation will come from a combination of factors. Let's take two businesses that on a like for like basis are quite similar from a product point of view. At the time of writing, a return flight from London Gatwick to Dublin (six days from now) with Ryanair was €177. With Aer Lingus, the fare was €188. Both flights were based on the same criteria: similar departure and return times, no checked in luggage, priority boarding not selected with Ryanair and no seats selected with either airline, and no insurance. If price was most important, then Aer Lingus should expect to fly with an empty aircraft. Yet in a recent survey, frequent flyers rated the Aer Lingus experience, while in some need of improvement, to be much more pleasant than Ryanair. Aer Lingus fares and loads are up according to their financial results!

Ryanair would argue that their prices are lower and that they have more on-time flights than any of their competitors. Undoubtedly that's often true. But why have they recently changed their strategy to become more customer-friendly and cuddly?

They openly acknowledge that not every passenger was happy with Ryanair restrictions, or to be bombarded with sales pitches for telephone cards and duty-free goods. Nor was every passenger happy to have to run to sit in unassigned seating with their partner, or to sit in a tight seat space, or to have a trumpet fanfare applauding the airline for doing what is expected – arrive on time.

This is not to pretend that Aer Lingus are fantastic. All airlines have room to improve. They give their frequent flyers points which are redeemable against free flights, but they take them away if they're not used within a certain timeframe. They are happy to bump you onto a different flight at no charge when the weather turns bad – and it suits them. However, if a frequent flying customer initiates the same request and asks to change a ticket to an earlier flight (having arrived an hour early and where the previous flight is not full), Aer Lingus will charge a fee. Those double standards are an irritant for frequent flyers who, with their membership cards, are clearly identifiable as regular customers.

Nevertheless, on a like for like basis, there are many that will opt for the green tube over the blue and yellow one, reinforcing the point that customers are motivated by a number of drivers – seldom by one only.

Look at the world of financial services. Banks sell mortgages. They will loan you an amount of money to buy a property at a given interest rate, frequency of repayment, term, etc., and with certain standard conditions. With respect to the banking world, there is not that much difference in mortgages among the various banks for a typical home. Yet banks all over the world try to attract new customers with a litany of product features and benefits. Where's the differentiation in that? There is none worth talking about. However, if a bank told you that they would simplify the process and flex with you to match your needs entirely, that might be a different story.

In the current world in which we operate, products and services are mere commodities. Customer experience in procuring these products and services is the true differentiator. With the advent of APIs and PSD2 (to name but a few) products and services can be 'plugged' into various platforms with ease. Solutions or customer experience experts will be the true merchant warriors of the future.

Like those merchants that braved the old silk road across ancient Asia, these new merchants equip themselves with a new geographical expertise. It is not knowledge of the physical journey across Asia but more simply 'Customer Journeys'. Instead of caravans, they use kanbans. The products and services already exist. They just need to be connected to the consumer in the simplest way possible, facilitating procurement and not pushing sales.

Cormac O'Brien, Head of Sales Quality Assurance, Bank of Ireland Retail

In a dynamic world, every organisation needs to find ways to differentiate. The argument here is that we have to think differently, as the old answers for differentiation might not suit a new future in your industry. While customer service is an ancient concept in a world of significant change, it hasn't gone away. In fact, experience shows that getting back to basics is more important than ever. Maybe the opportunities for differentiation are right in front of your nose... doing the basics right, day in and day out.

> *I have personally competed with Wal-Mart, so I know it can be done. You develop a uniqueness, a niche, and then you capitalise on it.*
> Don Soderquist, ex CEO of Ben Franklin Stores and later COO of Wal-Mart

The business case for premium service

Picture yourself and your partner in a nice restaurant. Let's pretend that the reputation of the restaurant is strong, the ambience and atmosphere is pleasant and relaxing, and the waiter is ultra professional. You order a nice bottle of wine which the waiter pours for you (after you taste it of course). When you are halfway down the glass, the waiter tops you up again. Isn't that great service?

The net effect is that you will usually drink more wine! More importantly, what's that doing to your check?

Make no mistake here – the waiter is like a 'wolf in sheep's clothing' – and good luck to that restaurant. After all, you get what you pay for. With this in mind, perhaps some managers should stop worrying about their sales targets! If they want to worry about something – let it be their customer satisfaction targets. If they deliver great service, that in itself will put money in the till.

Of course, this argument may not stack up in the boardroom. It's intended more as a piece of encouragement to help the manager prioritise the right things.

As mentioned earlier, *customer experience* is such a throw-away phrase that it's often not thought through fully or taken seriously. There are two ways of dismissing the cynics in the boardroom; by putting a financial value on giving great service, and by putting a value on getting it wrong. Let's first of all look at the risk of not taking it seriously.

Note: There is a lot of quantitative research in the public domain with percentages that seem to vary and conflict from survey to survey. In an attempt to present consensus here, don't get hung up on the actual percentage numbers that you're about to see. Don't worry – while the numbers may differ, the message in most of these surveys tends to be the same.

What if we get it wrong?

In all the billions of transactions that are taking place globally right now as you read this, regardless of the industry, an average 20% of them are going wrong. That means that one in five is going off track, to the point where the customer is somewhat upset. Of that 20% that are going wrong, only 4% of those people *actually* complain. The other 96% don't for varying reasons; they just couldn't be bothered... there are no obvious means of complaining... they don't believe that anything good will happen...

or they don't want to get the assistant in trouble. (These percentages and the reasons may vary in different cultures. Also, if the cost of the purchase or service is high, then it's likely that the number of customers complaining will be higher. The bottom line is that on average, most people just don't complain.)

Now it gets even more interesting of the 96% that don't complain, a scary 91% of *them* do not return. They simply defect and vote with their feet.

That means that on a global industry-wide average, organisations lose 17.5% (work it out, 91% of 96% of 20%) of their customers every year. If that is true for your business, you have to admit that you should re-think your strategy.

Here it is in table format:

All global transactions taking place right now	100%
What percentage is going wrong – to the point where customers are dissatisfied?	20%
What percentage of that 20% doesn't bother to complain?	96%
What percentage of that 96% doesn't come back?	91%
What is 91% of 96% of 20%? – **Defection Rate**	17.5%

What are the financial implications if those numbers were true for your business? Let's look at the pressure that would cause you.

Pretend that your sales last year were 100 and you plan to achieve, say, 7% growth this coming year. So your target for next year is 107. However, if the defection rate of 17.5% was true for your business, your last year base line slips from 100 to 82.5 (100-17.5). When you do the maths, you'll see that achieving a target of 107 from a base line of 82.5 requires growth of almost 30% (82.5 + 30% = 107).

Sales last year – 100	Planned growth for next year – 7%	Planned total therefore is 107

If the defection rate of 17.5% is real for your business,
then the base line of 100 slips to 82.5 (100 - 17.5 = 82.5)

New base line 82.5 (100 – 17.5)	Plus 7% growth =	87.75
New base line 82.5 (100 – 17.5)	Plus 30% growth =	107

So, which would you rather sign up to – a target of 7% or a target of 30%? It's a no-brainer, isn't it?

There is a further hint here. The defectors were also asked *why* they defected. Guess what... a massive 71% of them said it was due to the quality of their interaction – the service level they did or didn't get. Only 14% of the defectors said it was due to dissatisfaction with the product or price. (The remaining 15% was due to other uncontrollable elements such as attrition and competitor activity.)

Once again, don't let the accuracy of the percentages cloud your judgement here. You may have seen other surveys with other numbers, but the message will be the same.

If you do not prioritise service and if you get it wrong, you lose customers. That makes it harder for you to grow. Ask yourself: what is your defection rate? If you have a business where every customer is on a database (unlike most retailers), you can work it out and track it. If you have no current way of measuring it, use the generic 17.5% as a guideline and assume for now that it's the defection rate for your business.

Undoubtedly you have a strategy for getting new business, but what is your separate strategy for retaining your existing customers?

What if we get it right?

Let's flip this to a more positive angle. What if you *do* prioritise service and get it right? What's the commercial benefit? Does great customer experience really deliver sales? (The numbers here are for illustration purposes only and not based on actual research. You may insert different numbers but the message will stand out regardless.)

Let's take weekly grocery shopping as an example. Imagine if the average Tesco shopper is, say, 35, and stereotypically has a partner and two kids. Imagine also that their average spend is about €120 per week on groceries, which equates to €6,000 a year. That'll be for the next 40 years. You may argue that they will spend less when the kids move out. It's only partly true – the parents just buy more wine (for when the grandchildren come to visit)! Okay, so their spend might reduce slightly, but research shows that empty nesters tend to buy more premium products, thereby keeping their spend at the higher end of the scale.

Tesco Shopper – Sample

Average age of Tesco shopper	35
Average weekly spend	€120
Average annual spend (€120 x 50 weeks)	€6,000
For how many more years will they be spending at this rate?	40
Lifetime value (€6,000 x 40 years)	€240,000

So the lifetime value of this average Tesco customer is €240,000 (€6,000 pa for 40 years). Those customers are going to spend €240,000 somewhere. Remember that they have choices about where to spend it.

Imagine if you were working in that store and a customer approached you, asking you to help them spend €240,000 today, all in one go! What would you do? Of course you'd roll out the red carpet for them and treat them like royalty.

But why should they be treated any differently simply because they are taking 40 years to spend it? The reality is that as shoppers browse the aisles, they make several decisions about what to buy or what not to buy. But they also make a decision – even subliminally, as they walk out the door – as to whether they will return or not.

As a retailer and an executive of a trade association, I am frequently faced with the challenges of an increasingly competitive marketplace, made even more acute by an anaemic Lebanese economy. My brand, and many others, struggle to maintain the interest of fickle consumers, whose stagnating incomes are harder to part with. We cannot understand why sales fluctuate wildly. With all the trouble around it, Lebanon's is a rollercoaster economy.

To better understand these dynamics, and increase our abilities to face challenges, my association sought external support to help us appreciate the delicate balance between new technologies and the basics of profitable sales. We also learned how to drive footfall and convert browsers to buyers. We learned that, when times are tough, creating a unique shopping experience for our customers is a key to improved sales.

Raja Habre, Executive Director, Lebanese Franchise Association

Let's move away from retail and apply this to a different sector. We will use this simple model and apply it in a B2B world, such as a beverage wholesaler (bottled beers, minerals) who sells and delivers to publicans, hotels, clubs, and supermarkets. Here is what the example might look like in this industry. Assume an average weekly order value for a typical publican outlet is a nominal €1,000, which is €52,000 a year. Even with just a 10 year forecast, that equates to a lifetime value of €520,000. If you were a beverage wholesaler whose average order is €1,000, how would you treat a customer placing a single order for €520,000?

Beverage Wholesaler – Sample

Average weekly order value	€1,000
Average annual spend (€1000 x 52)	€52,000
Put a notional term on the life of the relationship	10
Lifetime value (€52,000 x 10 years)	€520,000

In the retail motor industry, an average customer changes their car every two to three years. A 35 year old customer that is buying one car today for €20,000 will also buy another 12–18 cars in their driving lifetime. That equates to a notional lifetime value of €300,000 (say 15 cars x €20,000). If you were a motor dealer and a customer wanted to buy 15 cars totalling €300,000 in one go, how would you treat them?

Motor Dealer – Sample

Average age of driver	35
Average value of motor car	€20,000
For how many more years will they be driving?	40
How frequently do owners change their car?	2-3 yrs
How many cars will they buy in that time?	15 approx
Lifetime value (€10,000 x 15)	€300,000

Doesn't this change how you might look at each customer from now on? Far too often customers are treated as *today customers* only, with no thought or value on future potential or spend. If everyone on your team thought of every customer as a *lifetime customer*, it would change behaviours instantly.

What is the *lifetime value* of your average customer? Work it out. This model can be applied to any sector, and it needs to be a way of thinking that is embedded in your culture.

Your Business

		You
What is your customer's average age? (If relevant)	A1	
What is your customer's average transaction value?	A2	
How frequently do they spend this amount?	A3	
What is their value per year (A2xA3)?	A4	
For how many more years are they likely to be a customer? (Refer to A1 if relevant)	A5	
Multiply **A4 x A5** to get the ***Lifetime Value*** of your customer	A6	

While many of the examples shown here are for tangible goods bought on the high street, the same messages apply to professional services and to goods sold business-to-business.

> *You've got to keep the customer satisfied.*
>
> Simon and Garfunkel

SUMMARY

To attract and retain customers, we need to tune in to what motivates customers to buy. When we've worked it out, we need to think about how we can differentiate ourselves from our competitors. It's difficult to do it on product or price alone. However, if we focus on the experience that our customers have while spending with us and make it great, that'll do it.

If it's so obvious and simple, why don't we do it all the time, and why doesn't everybody do it? There are a number of reasons, such as lack of prioritisation, lack of thought, complacency, culture, and poor systems and processes. Almost all of them can be eliminated with foresight and planning. It's mainly just common sense. Unfortunately, though, common sense is not always common practice.

Great service as an operating model is not discretionary – it is now a basic 'licence' for being in business. You simply have no choice. It is not by accident that some of the greatest businesses in the world put customer experience at the heart of what they do. Think of Wal-Mart, Selfridges, Harrod's, Disney, Emirates Airline, Four Seasons, Metro Bank... the list goes on.

Another consideration is that there is also an emotional reward for the individual that gives great service. Although many customers take it for granted, there are many more customers that really appreciate it and show their gratitude with a comment, a smile, a letter or whatever. One way or another, you will know when you have done a good job and you will feel good about it. It is quite motivational and personally rewarding to be nice.

As you travel through this book, you'll find a lot of references to the world of retail. The reason for that is that everyone knows retail, if only as a customer, and can therefore relate to it. Once the concepts, frameworks and examples are explained, it shouldn't take much to pick them up and adapt them to your own industry.

There are also certain common characteristics of best in the world retailers that you'll see repeated over and over.

Retailers are:

1. *Sophisticated yet practical*: Even with the best systems, technology and data, they still walk the floor to see for themselves how customers respond to a new product, a new display, a changed layout, etc.
2. *Very creative*: They continuously develop promotions, window displays and displays in store – all intended to entice you to spend
3. *Move at pace*: They have excellent technology to help make great decisions, yet a good merchant doesn't need technology to decide to push umbrellas out front as soon as it starts to rain
4. Experts at using *science, senses and theatre* in store to entertain, romance and sell in a way that many on-line retailers cannot do
5. *Very commercial*: They know how to drive footfall, convert browsers into spenders, and increase average spend

Finally, but most important of all, best in the world retailers are totally focused on the customer.

> *For my whole career in retail, I have stuck by one guiding principle. It's a simple one and I've repeated it over and over – the secret of success is giving great customer service.*
>
> Sam Walton – Wal-Mart Founder

Key Takeaways:

- Great service is now a basic ingredient for doing business – non-discretionary
- You need to differentiate your business – having consistently lowest prices and/or product differentiation is seldom enough or even possible
- Great customer experience is a proven business differentiator
- The business case for giving great customer experience is proven:
  - Think positively – think *lifetime value*
  - If you get it wrong, you risk having customers *defect* from you

Key Questions For You:

1. Is customer service on your radar?
2. What differentiates you from your competitors?
3. What is the *lifetime value* of your average customer?
4. What is your actual or estimated *customer defection rate*?
5. What are you doing about it?
6. How much of this have you communicated to your own people?

Watch For These Pitfalls:

- People and organisations often pay lip service to the concept of customer experience – so it becomes jargon
- There will be many obstacles to overcome, caused by a number of factors:
  - Resistance from people to change
  - Organisation culture doesn't support it
  - Other obstacles, real and perceived, caused by the organisation
- Lack of measurement leads to poor prioritisation

Chapter Two

What Is Premium Customer Experience in a New and Dynamic World?

What is meant by *great customer experience*? There are so many great answers – but how can they all be right? When asked to define great customer experience, people will often use personal anecdotes and definitions based on their own personal experiences, good and bad. Let's make sense of that here.

Here are some answers to the question in recent Kara workshops: The waiting time in a queue... no eye contact from a shop assistant... the speed of delivery of their order... the quality of the toast at breakfast... the lack of hot water in the rest room... the availability of a shoe in the correct size... the advice on how to cook fish... the unexpected offer of free alterations... the mulled wine on a cold day... the smile from the salesperson... etc.

Without doubt, these examples would influence your view and might help to shape your definition. The challenge for you is to work out which examples are important to your customers and which ones are less important.

If we look back at some of the arguments in the first chapter, where we saw that organisations simply *must* prioritise customer experience, here is a definition that may summarise what great customer experience is and why it is important:

> *Customer service is about doing whatever it takes... to ensure that your customer has a great experience... matching or exceeding their expectations... so that they*

> *spend as much as possible today... will be happy to come back... and recommend a friend.*
>
> Alan O'Neill – on a long-winded day!

Of course this definition is long-winded, but don't worry; you won't have to quote it too often. There is something much simpler coming shortly. The definition does, however, capture the true purpose and benefit of prioritising customer experience and will fit with almost any business.

The very basic requirement and starting point is to ensure that your offer at least matches your customer's initial expectation! It's simple – if customers have an expectation of a certain level of experience... and get that or more, of course they'll be satisfied and are likely to go back again and again. And indeed, they might recommend you to a friend.

While the anecdotes and examples of great customer experience expressed at the beginning of this chapter have value on their own or in a general conversation over a dinner party, they're just not strong enough when trying to communicate a message of ambition. Nor are they enough when communicating strategy or standards to your customers and employees. They simply won't remember an untidy list like that when presented without some order.

To define great customer experience for your business, you've got to be more structured than that. You've also got to think about communicating with and training your people, setting objectives... and indeed, how to measure service. Here is an effective framework and structure that will help almost every business.

3-legged stool – a framework for defining customer experience

Let's widen the debate and start thinking about customer experience at a different level, as *customer service* in some ways is too narrow a topic. As shown above, the purpose of giving great customer experience is to drive sales today, to ensure that customers return to spend tomorrow and that they recommend you to a friend. Customers will respond to this positively if their experience is favourable at all touchpoints. If it is not, then they are less likely to. We should think more holistically about the touchpoints where customers interact with your organisation and consider what that *experience* is like for them.

Let's take a side-step for a moment and picture a 3-legged stool. For a 3-legged stool to stand straight and upright, all three legs need to be in place. If one leg is missing, the stool will fall over. Worse again, imagine if two legs were missing... even an acrobat would struggle with that!

For a customer experience to be great, we have to think of the whole experience. The legs of the stool are represented by *Product*, *People* and *Place* (*place* referring to the physical environment). The three-legged-stool is a very effective analogy to use as a way of defining your customers' experience. It is simple and versatile and will work for all businesses. The concept is simple – if one 'leg of the stool' is missing, the customer's experience is less than it should be.

> *The customer experience is the next competitive battleground.*
> Jerry Gregoire, CIO, Dell Computers

For initial illustration purposes, let's take three B2C industries – hospitality, retailing and telephone networks – to explain the analogy.

Scenario 1 – Hospitality Sector

Picture yourself going to a really nice restaurant for a special meal. Imagine that the food is fantastic... it's hot, tasty, well-presented, fresh and interesting. So you might tick the box on *product*. Imagine too that the waiter is well groomed, efficient, friendly, knowledgeable and not over the top or 'in your face'. You might tick the box also on *people*. Imagine, however if the housekeeping standards are not up to scratch. Let's say that that there are crumbs on the seat and table on arrival. Maybe there are water stains on the glassware or cutlery, an unpleasant smell, no hot water in the restrooms, or the music is too loud. How then would you judge the overall experience?

Despite the great meal and professional waiter, you will leave with an iffy feeling about your experience. You may not articulate what was wrong as clearly as it's set out here, but you will have a somewhat negative feeling that will stay with you beyond the event and will influence your willingness to return or to recommend a friend.

> *I very much agree with this approach to creating a unique identity in order to make one's business successful. This can only be achieved through a positive customer experience. I believe that particularly in the service industry this customer experience has to be driven through the actions of the front-line employees. Strategy can be set at the top but if employees are well trained, motivated, empowered and properly rewarded, only then can they be relied upon to deliver the company strategy.*
> Gerald Lawless, Experienced Hotelier, including CEO of Jumeirah Group

Scenario 2 – Retail Sector

Imagine shopping in your local supermarket. If the *people* are great and the environment (*place*) is pristine, but some of the *products* are out of stock, that is a failure from your point of view as a customer. That negativity also applies to other product related issues, such as the range not being to your expectation, your desired brand not being stocked, prices being higher than competitors on a like for like basis, sizes and colour preferences being unavailable, or quality not being fit for purpose.

As with Scenario 1, if *product* is not to your satisfaction, you will have a somewhat negative feeling that will stay with you beyond the event and will influence your willingness to return or to recommend a friend.

Scenario 3 – Telephone Network Provider

Organisations are so often let down by their front line staff through rudeness and other inappropriate behaviours. Imagine a scenario where you call your telephone company to change to a different tariff on your telephone bill. For this scenario, imagine the waiting time before a real person speaks to you (*place*) is short and easy (unlikely however!!). Then pretend that you are offered a tariff option (*product*) that matches your needs, but the operator is rude, impatient, dismissive or over-familiar with you. You will feel let down and not happy.

As with the two previous scenarios, if the *people* element is not to your satisfaction, you will have a somewhat negative feeling that will stay with you beyond the event and will influence your willingness to return or to recommend a friend.

These are serious but practical considerations, regardless of the industry you measure yourself against. It's not that you take out a checklist and tick boxes after your encounters but you would certainly get a feeling of some dissatisfaction in any of the three scenarios presented here. They would affect either your likelihood to return or how you might feel if you do return. Or indeed, your willingness to give a positive recommendation of that service provider to a friend.

Customers' experiences should match their basic expectations at the very least. The customer will have expectations in each of the Ps, whether we like it or not. Two Ps out of three is not good enough – never mind one P out of three!

By the way, this is not an attempt to change the language from *customer service* to *customer experience*. That's too big a challenge. As long as you and your team understand the wider context, that is all that matters.

Perhaps some might argue that the three legs have varying priorities. That may also be true. At different times and for different customers, the effects of each might vary. But how do you know for sure? Anyway, that's creating complexity out of simplicity. Because you can't always know, it's better to get all three 'Ps' as near to perfect as possible, consistently.

Although obviously very similar, these 3 Ps should not be confused with the 4 Ps of marketing (Product, Price, Promotion and Place). The 3 Ps here (Product, People, Place) are shown specifically to help shape the customer experience. The 4 Ps of marketing (Product, Price, Promotion and Place) are to help define a wider strategy. One of those 4 Ps (Price) that you're used to using is absorbed into Product here in the 3-legged stool for simplicity. Remember, this 'stool' will be used as a framework to communicate your service standards to all your employees, where most of them have no control over *price* in the first place. So let's keep it simple.

How do the 3 Ps work for B2B industries other than B2C retailers and hotels?

If you are a distribution company, contact centre, or some other organisation where you are taking your business to the customers rather than them coming to you, the interpretation of *Place* changes and refers to something else. (*Product* and *People* stay the same.)

For distribution companies, *Place* can refer to your route to market or your distribution channel, which includes such things as delivery schedules, calibre of trucks, ordering system, etc. Similarly, if you are a contact centre, *Place* refers to your telephone or on-line system and process. Use and adapt it in whatever way suits you. It's a framework, after all, not a definitive list.

As presented above, the 3-legged stool is a model that will help you determine the experience your customers will have when they interact with you. How can it work effectively, given that within each industry there are often different levels of service both expected and delivered? Take the extreme example of Four Seasons Hotels contrasted with a 'greasy spoon' type cafe. In both establishments you can get fed, yet their service offerings are poles apart and at opposite ends of the service spectrum. How can the 3-legged stool (3 Ps) still work for both?

> *Our experience in ifac working with Irish food and agribusinesses strongly suggests that excellent customer experience in a B2B environment is critical to success. Spending time on your customer journey to reduce friction in the buying experience for example, or to help your customer have a great experience throughout their engagement with you – will deepen loyalty and improve profitability. Building this customer centric culture in an organisation is key and it's why this book is very timely.*
>
> David Leydon, Head of Food and Agri Business, ifac

The difference is in the detail. For example, let's contrast Four Seasons Hotels and the Corner Shop Cafe. In Four Seasons Hotels, you will be given silver cutlery and linen napkins (*Place*). In Corner Shop Cafe, you are likely to get paper napkins and plastic cutlery. In The Four Seasons you will get a main course of fresh ingredients from a wide menu, freshly cooked to your taste and served to your table (*Product*). In Corner Shop Cafe, you might queue to get a set offering from a set menu with limited flexibility to suit your taste. And that is okay! Why? Because that offer is consistent with the Corner Shop Cafe proposition, or *its* brand DNA.

Brand DNA – linked to level of service

The key difference in your service offering should be determined by the DNA of your brand. Brand is often 'owned' and seen as a marketing department thing. Yes, marketing have a role to play in perhaps facilitating its creation, design and development – in addition to a key role, which is to use effective, consistent and relevant messaging to drive footfall. A clearly articulated brand DNA will guide them along the way, but it also sets the direction and the tone for the rest of the business to comply with and follow.

However as outlined earlier, customers' willingness to purchase, to return and to recommend to a friend is mainly influenced by the experiences they have. Therefore, brand DNA should set the context and inform all issues to do with *product, people, place, processes, resource allocation, processes and behaviours* – and is the responsibility of the whole company.

In the worlds of B2B and B2C, the 3-legged stool provides you with a set of questions. Here are some samples:

Product	People	Place
• What level of quality and pricing? • What range of sizes, packs, colours and style? • Etc.	• How many front-line people should we have? • How should they be dressed? • What behaviours do we expect? • Etc.	• What quality of kit and presentation? • What is the delivery schedule? • Etc.

The answers are determined by who you want to be as a brand – your brand DNA.

Communication of that DNA is critical. Employees need to know about it, and what it means to them. Their actions and behaviours should be defined and then measured against it. (See later chapters on Culture and Measurement.)

Brand DNA is the core reference point and umbrella for every business – business to business (B2B), business to customer (B2C) and public sector. It should be a context and reference point for all decisions and actions. If it is not proactively thought out and planned for, it will evolve by default anyway, which might be good or bad. Employees and customers will then form opinions and perceptions based on their actual experiences. Every business needs to have a blueprint, and a carefully thought-out brand DNA will help to do just that. But it's got to be consistent. For example, Fedex promise *on-time overnight delivery*. It would be a recipe for disaster if they regularly failed on that promise and they would soon lose credibility.

Brands are often echoed in Vision and Mission Statements. These should not just be tag lines and logos. Be sure that you all agree on what you can be passionate about and what can drive your financial performance. In his book *Good to Great*, Jim Collins talks about the *Hedgehog Principle*:

> Regardless of what clever antics the fox gets up to in trying to catch the hedgehog – the 'stupid hedgehog' just rolls up into a ball every single time. It never deviates from its core 'modus operandi' despite the myriad of different challenges and opportunities it faces.

Once your Brand DNA (your hedgehog) is defined and accepted, you've got to stay resolutely focused on it and not allow any of your team to deviate from that.

Here are some sample promises from some of the world's best known companies. The statements are a clear declaration of intent by each respective organisation and help to shape their service levels. On their own, though, they are not enough. Behind the scenes, each will most likely have a set of guiding principles that give employees further clarity around what is expected. For those you recognise, do you think they deliver on their promises?

Company	Brand promise
Amazon	To be Earth's most customer centric company; to build a place where people can come to find and discover anything they might want to buy online.
Ann Summers	We will be the global authority and destination for pleasure. We will inspire our customers to look and feel sexy – with innovative, fun and daring experiences.
Apple	Apple is committed to bringing the best personal computing experience to students, educators, creative professionals and consumers around the world through its innovative hardware, software and Internet offerings.
Bharti Airtel	To be the most loved brand – enriching the lives of millions.
Cash & Carry Kitchens	We will be Ireland's favourite destination for fitted kitchens and wardrobes – with a reputation for great service, quality and value
Disney	To be the leading entertainment company in the world... to protect and develop the Disney name... to foster a culture of quality, imagination and service.
Dubai Duty Free	Provide customers with first class customer service, excellent value for money, a wide range of quality products and a world class shopping environment.
Four Seasons	To specialise within the hospitality industry by offering only experiences of exceptional quality. Our objective is to be recognised as the company that manages the finest hotels, resorts and residence clubs wherever we locate.
General Motors	To be the world leader in transportation products and related services... thorough continuous improvement... driven by integrity, teamwork and innovation.
Google	To organize the world's information and make it universally accessible and useful.
Harrod's	We will be the most trusted iconic brand in the world for exceptional luxury experiences.
HJ Heinz	Dedicated to the sustainable health of people, the planet and our Company.
Irish Inland Revenue	To serve the community by fairly and efficiently collecting taxes and duties and implementing Customs controls.

Continued

Continued

Company	Brand promise
McDonald's	To be the world's best quick service restaurant experience. Being the best means providing outstanding quality, service, cleanliness, and value, so that we make every customer in every restaurant smile.
Microsoft	To enable people and businesses throughout the world to realize their full potential.
Nike	To bring inspiration and innovation to every athlete in the world.
Selfridges	To be *the* destination for the most extraordinary customer experience.
Southwest Airlines	Dedication to the highest quality of Customer Service delivered with a sense of warmth, friendliness, individual pride, and Company Spirit.
Tesco	Creating value for customers, to earn their lifetime loyalty.
Wal-Mart	To help people save money so they can live better.

Organisations regularly mix and confuse their Vision and Mission Statements. To simplify it, see the Vision as an inward target and aspiration to aim for in the future, whereas the Mission Statement is your external purpose and *how* you intend to deliver your Vision. Both are important and should be linked.

Vision – *To be the destination for the most extraordinary customer experiences*

Mission – *We are here to surprise, amaze and amuse our customers – and everyone is welcome*

Selfridges, UK

Vision – *We will be the industry's favourite and most trusted resource for fresh produce*

Mission – *We will support our customers with premium quality produce, innovation and consistently great service*

Donnelly Fresh Foods, Ireland

The compelling reason for your customers to come back for more is your brand's consistent ability to deliver distinctive and relevant experiences at all touchpoints. So where do you start in developing your brand? Here are a few thoughts to remind you of some considerations in developing or revisiting your own brand DNA:

1. What would you like your key stakeholders (owner, team, customers, competitors, suppliers, media) to be saying about you in five years' time?
2. What perception do you want to create in your employees and customers?
3. What is your brand promise?

4. What are the core values of your brand that guide your behaviours and business practices?
5. What are your brand's distinctive advantages (i.e. your USP – Unique Selling Proposition)?
6. Can you leverage your brand's USP?
7. What compelling reasons will your customers have to buy from you?
8. What compelling reasons are there for your own people to be passionate about your brand and really get behind it?
9. What standards of performance excellence will you demand from your people, your processes and your financials?
10. Can you be the best in your market segment?
11. Can you make money from it? Is it commercially viable?

Determining the appropriate level of service, linked to your brand DNA and competitive positioning

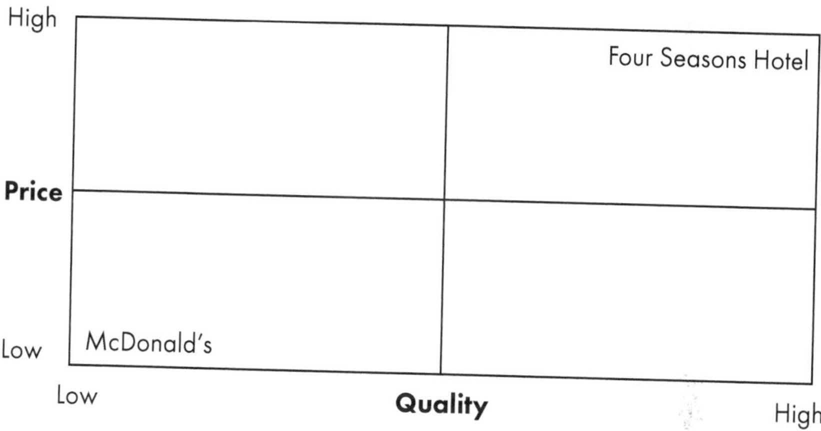

To further help you define your brand DNA, and as a quick visual way to communicate it internally, plot your business in a price/service quality matrix, like this:

For illustration purposes:

Generally speaking, in the airline industry, Emirates Airline would be in the top-right-hand corner, and Ryanair would be in the middle bottom. Four Seasons would be to the right in the top-right-hand quadrant, and McDonald's in contrast would be in the left of the bottom-left-hand one. That is not to say that McDonald's is poor quality, but when compared to Four Seasons (in fairness to this exercise), it is in a different league.

If you were to do the same exercise for the *fast food* industry only – where Four Seasons has no place in that matrix – McDonald's might be positioned in the top-right-hand corner against a 'greasy spoon' cafe in the bottom-left-hand corner.

How to use this for your business:

Start by listing all the main competitors in your sector that you care about. Take the most prominent competitor (but not yourself for now – even if that is you). Rate that competitor on both scales, *product* and *quality*, and put their initials in the appropriate quadrant. For example, if competitor AB-Co score 6 on price and 4 on quality, then put AB in the top-left-hand quadrant. Now, using that first competitor as a baseline, complete the exercise and measure all other competitors against that baseline. Leave your own organisation to last. Plot them and yourself in the matrix to get a visual picture of your competitive set.

What does it tell you? Are you happy with where you sit right now, or are you a 'me-too' offer in the middle of a cluttered space? Are your competitors better differentiated and positioned than you? Does it prompt you to re-think your offer for differentiation purposes?

What if others did the same exercise about you in your absence? How would your customers or competitors rate you? Would they rate you the same way as you did yourself?

If this hasn't given you some food for thought already, perhaps you need to eat some humble pie and do the exercise again.

> *I have been up against tough competition all my life. I wouldn't know how to get along without it.*
>
> Walt Disney

As the world continues to change at an exponential and explosive rate, your competitors and your customers are also changing. The technology revolution in particular has made the world a very small place indeed. Customers can now compare specifications and prices right across the world. The cost of entry has also come down for many products and industries. With that globalisation, it is more difficult than ever to differentiate on product alone.

Organisations everywhere are looking for other ways to differentiate, and many believe they can do it through excelling in customer experience. Because that is true, it means that you have to go even further with your customer experience levels.

Now consider where your optimum new position should be in the matrix. Do you need to make more changes? When you're clear and happy on where you wish to sit in the matrix, you could use this for internal communications as a tool and motivator for your teams. This could also be used to great effect in a sales meeting with a customer, where you illustrate your USP very simply and visually.

Know that there is a global movement, and organisations the world over are trying to improve their propositions. Premium market positioning is growing, and that will expose those that are not matching customer expectations. You simply *have no choice* but to improve your proposition. As you read this, your competitors are having similar thoughts and conversations about this topic, and they too recognise the need to improve their proposition. Doing nothing differently is, in effect, going backwards. Now consider where your optimum position is in the matrix. Do you need to make some changes that will kick ass and give you a significant stretch ahead of the competition?

In any event, this Competitive Positioning Matrix and your Vision and Mission will set a tone and context for your 3 Ps, or your service proposition. These become the North Star for your business. They'll provide a framework and context for every department in your organisation.

The matrix is shown here as a generic high-level exercise for now, but it is best used in detailed planning. For example, do the exercise at the next level down, i.e. do it just for *product*, again for *people* and again for *place*. It will help you significantly to think differently about opportunities for differentiation.

'Customer service' used to mean literally serving customers well, which resulted in repeat business. Lately, this has evolved into service efficiency, which in many cases, skips the personal interaction. We're old school in Harley-Davidson Dublin! We work to create an experience which will delight our visitors.

We employ team members who, above all, want to be here and enjoy the experience also. Processes are of course learned and executed, but never hidden behind. Every interaction has the goal of strengthening the relationship with our visitors, which will result in repeat business and sincere referral. That is the only true CSI.

Jeff Murphy, Managing Director, Dublin Harley-Davidson

What level of customer experience is right for your business?

So far, we have identified the 3-legged stool as a framework and structured way of defining how your customer experience should be made up. Used effectively, the 3 Ps will help you develop a complete set of questions to be asked to help you define your customers' experience. The answers to those questions will come partly from who you are as an organisation, or your brand DNA.

Let's not forget that there are other ingredients that also feed into and determine *what good looks like*. They are to do with the available profit margin from your product mix. For example, if your brand aspiration and ambition is to deliver your product with bells and whistles, but the cost of the bells and whistles eats up the margin, of course that won't work. The ideas and models presented here need to enable you to make money! Additionally, who are your customers? What are their reasonable expectations?

The answers to *what good looks like* for you should come from these questions:

1. What is my brand DNA?
2. Who are my customers, and what are their reasonable expectations?
3. What can I differentiate with in each of the 3 Ps?
4. Can I make money from delivering on this?

Your customers will influence this too

Regardless of whether your customer base is mass market or niche market, be careful. Wal-Mart is the largest physical store discount retailer in the world and their target base is the mass market. Yet everyone, including the rich, likes a bargain. Rich people shopping in a Wal-Mart store know, however, that they won't be offered a glass of champagne like they were on their last first-class flight with American Airlines. Nor do they expect it from Wal-Mart.

If your target audience is niche market, you'd better know their needs and wants. But that has to be coupled with what is relevant to your brand and your competitive environment in the first place. You won't get linen napkins in McDonald's, and you won't get plastic cutlery in Four Seasons.

Rather than making assumptions, go and ask your customers, or at least observe them. Don't just use general loose questions, or you'll get answers similar to those given in the Kara workshop at the top of this chapter. Using the 3-legged stool as a framework, ask questions under each P that are relevant to your competitive environment. This research can be done at zero cost and with just a little forward planning.

What does good look like for your customers?

When you have agreed on your brand DNA, your customer profiles and your margin expectation, you will find that the detail for each leg of the stool will fall into place. The 3 Ps merely provide a set of questions relevant to your business and the answers will be guided by your brand DNA.

You still have to do the work, which entails internal research and brainstorming as well as the external customer observations or research referred to earlier. Using the framework of the 3-legged stool, why not run a series of internal workshops to involve your team and get them to propose what is right for your business? To repeat: this should be informed and influenced by your brand DNA and competitive differentiation, your customers' needs and wants, and of course, your margin requirement.

Each of the Ps is detailed in following chapters, but here are some sample thoughts to keep in mind for now:

People:

Number	Grooming standards	Calibre and attitude
Roles	Behaviours	Knowledge and skills

Product:

Mix	Stock levels	Brands
Price architecture	Exclusivity	Newness

Place:

Housekeeping	Merchandising	Lighting, ticketing, etc.
Supply chain	Deliveries	Other sensory things, like smell, touch, sound, etc.

This is not meant to be an exhaustive list, but simply a sample guide. If we return to the Four Seasons and McDonald's comparison, you'll notice that the questions are the same, but the answers would be different. For example, what chicken dish? Four Seasons would say *Beggar's Chicken wrapped in clay*, and McDonald's would say *deep-fried chicken nuggets*.

To explain this model in a hotel, we have so far only focused on the restaurant. The menu and dining element of the Four Seasons is only part of the customer experience, however. The same 3-legged stool framework should also be applied to each significant interaction: the booking, check-in, concierge, bedrooms, bar, conference facilities, leisure centre/spa, and check out.

Using the same model, let's apply it to other industries. Here are some specific examples:

Food Distributor:

People:

Number	Behaviours	Calibre
Roles	Frequency of sales rep call	Knowledge and skills

Product:

Mix	Stock levels	Packaging
Price architecture	Size options	Promotions

Place:

Delivery schedules	Ordering process	Telephone guidelines
Delivery van	Depot standards	Paperwork

Law Practice:

People:

Number	Calibre	Advice
Roles	Behaviours	Knowledge and skills

Product/Services:

Probate	Taxation	Commercial matters
Family matters	Conveyancing	

Place:

Office housekeeping	Print collateral	Telephone guidelines
Correspondence		

Airline:

People:

Number	Grooming	Calibre and attitude
Roles	Behaviours	Knowledge and skills

Product:

Routes and timings	Services on board	Entertainment
Price architecture	Exclusivity and newness	

Place:

Check-in and queues	Club lounge	Seating
Announcements	Housekeeping	Baggage handling

Rules, processes and resources

The 3-legged stool helps to define the customer experience, but rules and processes also have a role to play. They're usually decided centrally at management level. They also need to support the customer experience relevant to customer expectations and be conducive to industry benchmarks and your brand DNA.

Take refunds, for example. Notwithstanding the laws and statutory rights in your country with regard to refunds, some companies make it really difficult to get a refund. Their processes are designed with the company's needs at the forefront rather than the customer's needs. One of the airlines mentioned earlier will agree to a refund under duress. But to get it, you have to call their 'customer service' department at very specific hours. You pay premium rate for the phone call and are kept hanging on while the process determines which buttons you press. By the time you get to the third or fourth pressing of a button, your stress level is rising and you're probably ready to throw the telephone out the window!

Sufficient resources such as people, money and time also need to be appropriately allocated relevant to your brand positioning. If you go to Aldi or Lidl, you don't expect any help (*people*) in the aisles, as that is not their business model. You know that before you go in because you know theirs is a discount model: low prices, therefore low costs. Ryanair talk about a 'no frills' policy as that is their model. But even Tesco are realising lately that they may have cut staff numbers too far, as it is affecting the customer experience relevant to *their* model. Similarly, if Four Seasons don't spend the money on plush seating and provide plastic hard chairs instead, that is an obvious mismatch with their brand.

When this collision of rules, process, resources and supposed customer experiences don't match, it just doesn't make sense. It also sends a confused message to your customers. The challenge therefore for the policy makers in the organisation is to stand back and think about the whole customer experience. Too often, senior managers criticise the front line for poor service – when often it is the policies, rules and resources that the front-line have to work to that cause the problem.

SUMMARY

There are numerous definitions for what customer service actually is. This chapter has introduced a framework to help you define customer service and get it right for your business. The 3-legged stool, represented by *Product, People* and *Place*, is a superb tool to help you communicate your expectations to your own people and then measure against that.

Because the tool is so versatile, it will work for almost any industry and for organisations at all levels within that sector. This is where you also need to consider your positioning in a differentiated marketplace. For example, the 3-legged stool will work for a motor dealer regardless of whether they are selling Mercedes or Hyundai. Clearly both brands are poles apart in terms of price and quality. Therefore, the Competitive Positioning Matrix should be used in conjunction with the stool. The stool provides a possible set of questions; your desired positioning in the matrix will provide the answers to those questions.

Key Takeaways:

- The 3-legged stool framework will work as a customer service template for almost every business
- For B2C companies where the customer comes to them, it's about *Product, People, Place*
- For B2B organisations that take their business to the customer, *Place* infers *Route to Market*

- The Competitive Positioning Matrix will help you think about your best positioning and help identify your USPs
- Clearly defined Vision and Mission statements act as a North Star for a business – provided they don't just end up as a framed picture on the wall of reception!

Key Questions For You:

- Where do you sit in your Competitive Positioning Matrix – currently?
- Where do you aspire to be in the future?
- How can you make the 3 Ps relevant for your business?
- What is your USP under each of the 3 Ps?
- What 'star rating' do you want to be? Be realistic – we can't all be five star!

Watch For These Pitfalls:

- Give respect to your competition – they may be better than you think
- Do not make assumptions about *what good looks like*, find out for sure
- List the full detail for each element of *Product*, *People* and *Place* at all touchpoints in the customer journey

Part Two

What Is Premium Customer Experience in Detail?

Chapter Three

Deliver Premium Through Product

This chapter builds on *product* as introduced in the previous chapter and provides some detail to help further your understanding. The point has already been made that in this world of globalisation and lowering of barriers to entry, differentiation is difficult to achieve on product alone. However, product is important. It is the backbone to what drives business and profitability for most organisations. What are the things you need to consider to make you relevant for your market segment?

As a basic and fundamental ingredient, care is needed regarding the quality of your product or service. If you decide that your brand DNA and your margin expectation determine that you sell your product at a low price, that doesn't mean customers will be happy to pay for poor quality. Just because customers are paying less doesn't mean that they'll put up with sub-standard, or product that is not fit for purpose. And the funny thing is, those customers can often be the first ones to complain if something goes wrong.

A recent example highlighted this. An in-company contract caterer won the business with their corporate client on price alone. In order to fulfil the contract and still make a profit, they had to provide a food menu that was of a lower standard than the previous provider. Over time, the client and the contract caterer had endless complaints from the users of the service. Needless to say, their contract wasn't renewed.

Product – What does good look like?

There are some age-old sayings that apply to product, such as:

- Product needs to be fit for purpose
- Customers expect the right product, at the right price, in the right place at the right time

> *It does exactly what it says on the tin.*
> Ronseal TV Advertisement

Customers need choice while businesses need sales. Retailers marry the two needs by focusing on price architecture: *good, better and best.* For example, a cookshop won't just stock one model of frying-pan. They might stock Prestige (*good* entry price level), Stellar (*better* or mid price level), and Fissler (*best* – premium range). By having this wide range of prices, they'll appeal to a wider customer audience. This also makes it easier for the salesperson to up-sell to all customer types.

The product in a restaurant is the meal itself – starting with the menu theme, choice, quality and price. Interestingly, hoteliers often refer to the overall hotel brand as 'the product'. In this book, however, we take that down to the next level by describing the product detail in the bar, product selection in the restaurant, etc.

For a hotel, the *product* and *place* often overlap. For example, are the bedrooms, conference facilities and bar to be classified under *product* or *place*? Don't bother giving it even one more minute's thought. The 3 Ps have already done their job for you by getting you to even think it through. Put them wherever you like. One client, for example, classified their bar as the product, as it was a well-known music venue in its own right and a significant attraction for the hotel.

If you're an fmcg distributor, your product is whatever it is, say dairy products for the sake of this example. But you need to be mindful of having pack sizes fit for purpose, clear labelling, appropriate promotions, exclusives, regular newness and so on. Be careful too of out-of-stocks. Obviously you'll try to keep them to a minimum, but operational things do go wrong, causing out-of-stocks to happen. In such cases, your challenge moves to one of communication, such as informing customers at time of ordering that a product is out of stock. As you manage their expectations, they'll appreciate and respect you for it.

In a recent Kara customer survey on behalf of an fmcg distributor, customers were asked to comment on out-of-stocks. It was interesting to see that while they understood that out-of-stocks can happen from time to time, lack of communication in advance of the delivery was unforgivable.

If a retailer is listing your product and has space allocated on the shelf, there is nothing more damaging for your brand than an empty shelf. That damage is done to you, the retailer and the consumer. However, if you communicate the stock position in a timely way, the retailer can plan to temporarily replace that out-of-stock item with another product.

There is a lot to consider in determining *what good looks like* for your product relative to your desired market positioning. But there is a check-list. Let's expand on product some more with a check-list to help you determine *what good looks like* for your business.

Flagships and category killers

Differentiation is important for every business. But in a world where the barriers for entry, globalisation and speed to market are changing in favour of more competition, how can you develop differentiation in product? How can you ensure your product is not just a commodity? How can you develop a USP with your product?

Clearly, global brands have done this very effectively. Disney, BMW, GE... the list goes on. After years of huge investment, many of them have succeeded. But what if you are an organisation without the resources of the big names? Is it still possible to differentiate?

It is worth borrowing some old ideas from great retailers and applying them to your own business. By developing *flagships* and *category killers*, you will have the opportunity to differentiate without needing to rob the bank to do so.

A *flagship* is a single point destination for a brand that has authority and leadership in its market (think Louis Vuitton on the Champs-Elysees in Paris, or Apple on Regent Street in London). These iconic brands ensure that they have a stand-alone presence in major cities. As flagships, these locations make a profound statement for that brand. The brand will usually invest heavily in this site to make that strong presence and statement.

A *category killer* is where an organisation has developed an authority and is the best edit or destination for a category of product/service, or indeed a sector of the market. For example, when Nokia were at the top of their game, they *owned* the global mobile telephone market. The opportunity here is one of ownership in a chosen category, which is about having real authority for that category.

Here is an example of both flagships and category killers applied to a city. Imagine if you were the marketer for New York City and your job was to drive tourism footfall to the city. Given that there is lots of competition on the East Coast of the US, as a marketer you'd have to think about differentiation. Of course, there is much to make NYC stand out, enough to fill many books. For the purpose of this exercise, what has it got?

Apart from great shopping, which of course you will also find in other US cities, what has NYC got that is unique and iconic? Its flagship destinations include the Empire State Building, Rockefeller Center, Central Park, the Statue of Liberty, and the Ground Zero Memorial Site. From a category killer perspective, NYC has Broadway, which is the destination for stage shows in the US, and it also has amazing shopping. As the marketer for NYC, what are you going to shout about? Clearly you have lots of focus points to differentiate you.

Hotel Example

A hotel on the east coast of the UK took this message, invested in it and developed their fantastic spa as a flagship destination with a leading skincare product brand – i.e. *flagship destination*. Also, because they already have a great wedding business, they have developed it and taken that a stage further to blow their competitors out of the water – by making weddings a *category killer*. When it comes to customer messaging, this hotel ought to shout about what they *own* and have as a USP. That will drive footfall to their respective destinations. It gives them a point of difference, something different to say, and it builds customer confidence. In this example, customers that were enticed by the spa and/or weddings will spend money on other things too, such as the bar and restaurant.

Accountancy Profession Example

Most average accountancy firms earn revenue from end-of-year accounting and audits. One practice majors in tax advice, more than you'd get from a regular practice. While their core business is 'end of year accounting', they can also differentiate through specialist tax advice and use that for messaging their point of difference.

Another very successful small practice has cornered the market in their region for being experts in the hospitality industry, where they have developed specialist sectoral expertise. This is a twist on the *category killer* concept, where they *own* a target customer segment.

Retail Bank Example

Retail banks sell financial products in all shapes and sizes and for all sorts of financial needs. Whether it is a home loan, a car loan, a current or savings account, or a credit card, there is not that much difference between one high street bank's products and the next. Some may have special brand names, and terms and rates may differ slightly. But the reality is that most banks will acknowledge that their products are a commodity. How can they differentiate with category killers?

Having leadership in any product means that customers of the product are more likely to at least include the market leader in their thinking when they go to buy. AIB Bank in particular is a key player for mortgages in Ireland. They don't have that leadership by accident, as they have identified the opportunity and developed it. It makes perfect strategic sense for AIB, because mortgages are a key driver of other banking business, such as mortgage protection, other insurance policies and current accounts. Customers are inclined to put most of their personal business through the same bank that holds their mortgage, so this is good business for any bank.

Convenience Store Retailer Example

By definition and by their very existence, convenience stores are designed to be small, efficient and easily accessible. The number of product lines and the amount of stock will naturally be much smaller than a supermarket. Imagine, for example, the selection of breads in a convenience store compared to a supermarket. The choice will be much reduced. But category killers are still possible.

BWG Foods in Ireland own and manage the Spar, Mace and Londis brands in a franchise operating model. Mace in particular have about 160 stores in all sorts of geographic locations. Because local competition may vary, a single category killer doesn't make sense for the whole estate. The concept of category killers might be localised for each store. For example, one Mace store has identified fresh flowers to be an opportunity for differentiation. There is no flower shop locally, and they have the space, the interest and the skill to 'own' flowers in their area. The margin and the volume potential might not be fantastic, but it does give that Mace store a point of difference and a story to tell. Flowers can become a footfall driver for them.

An example from the world of B2B: housewares

The housewares industry in the UK has seen a lot of rationalisation in recent years. Ten years ago, there were many specialist distributors that specialised in their respective categories, such as T&G Woodware for woodware, Fissler for cookware, and so on. However, over the years, as the trade faced difficulties, many distributors branched out into related product categories. Because they each had strong relationships with their respective customers, they decided to capitalise on those relationships to sell more diversified product. Many of them ended with up with a much diluted offer and lost their original core.

Throughout all this change, T&G Woodware also spread their wings to include other product categories such as ceramics, acrylic, melamine and marble. However, they stayed true to their original identity, which was and still is woodware. Despite a much expanded product portfolio and a changed industry, T&G still 'own' the woodware category in the industry.

It might not always be possible to have a *flagship* product/brand/service in your portfolio. But you should certainly be able to identify a *category killer*.

Flagships and category killers give you key messages that stand you out from your competition and enable you to *own* something as a USP. It doesn't mean that you don't also have other core products or services. That may well be where your main business comes from. However, *core* does not give you a strong enough story to tell. If all you have is core, then you risk being a 'me too' in product.

> *A lot of companies have chosen to downsize, and maybe that was the right thing for them. We chose a different path. Our belief was that if we kept putting great products in front of customers, they would continue to open their wallets.*
>
> Steve Jobs

Exclusivity and newness

In the ongoing effort to differentiate, organisations in all sectors will try to have some element of exclusivity. That might be a new concept, a new idea, a way of working, a celebrity endorsement, a new promotion, a new advertisement or catchphrase, whatever message might make them stand out. The notion of being the only 'go to' place is not in itself new or novel, but it is a superb idea.

There was a time when only wealthy consumers could afford a Louis Vuitton bag, but now you'll see these bags on the arms of many people of all levels of wealth. Even less well-off people, who in the past might have found such brands to be beyond their means, will aspire to and then find a way to own one. In an age where accessibility has been made easier and class distinction is eroding, brands know that their appeal is widening.

Nevertheless, they will not flood the market and make their products available on every street corner. Selling an LV bag is only available for the elite retailers. Because of their appeal and because they drive footfall, premium department stores will do whatever it takes to secure LV as a partner in their stores.

For organisations that distribute branded products, their buyers are going to the same trade shows, reading the same magazines and researching in a similar way to their competitors. Your competitors are also looking for exclusivity, probably for the same products or brands as you. Getting exclusivity of major brands and opportunities is therefore becoming more difficult as the power shifts to the brands themselves. They often decide who they will give their brand or products to. In such cases, the best you might do is to get exclusivity for the launch of a new product for a short period of time only. That is still worth doing.

The world of product development has changed dramatically in the last hundred years. The years from 1900 to 1960 were dominated by manufacturing and product innovation. For example, at that time there were only a few global washing powder brands. Exclusivity was possible while the competitive world caught up. Now, as technology and globalisation has advanced so much, innovation and disruption has enabled a steady stream of newness, in every walk of life.

Change is constant, and that shows in the constant ebb and flow of new products and new fashions. This whets the consumer's appetite and has probably educated and groomed the consumer to tire more quickly and more easily. Organisations can resist it or adapt to it, but it's a reality. If you haven't prioritised newness in whatever field you're in, you may be missing a trick.

> 1. *Beauty had been 'on fire', due to a number of exclusive products.*
>
> 2. *There were over 40 different bespoke solutions in store, which you could only find here. It set us apart as a destination.*
>
> Anne Pitcher – MD of Selfridges UK

If you are a manufacturer and are developing your own products, how often do you prioritise innovation and newness? What is different about your product? If it's just a 'me-too' product, you will not displace the competition and get customers to change. Why should they?

Price architecture

Price architecture is where an organisation will have a range of products or services at various price levels in order to have a wider appeal. In simplest terms and using classic retail language, it's known as 'good, better and best'. For example, a restaurant serving lunches might have a choice of sandwiches (good), a salad offer (better) and a hot meal choice (best). They'll do this to create choice and not lose a customer to a competitor. Obviously, they would like if every customer ordered a hot meal, which is top price. But they also know that if they do that, they might alienate the customer who just wants a sandwich or a salad.

Your brand positioning will determine the actual price levels at each band. For example, a local pub might have a sandwich for €5 (good), a salad offer for €10 (better) and a hot meal for €15 (best). But a five star hotel is more likely to have a sandwich at €10 (good), a salad offer for €15 (better) and a hot meal for €20 (best). The brand DNA of a five star hotel is understandably positioned differently to a local three or four star pub.

Notice the concept is the same – the difference, however, is the average selling price.

This concept will work for your business too, whether you are B2C or B2B. Here are some more examples:

Company or product	Good	Better	Best
Cash and Carry Kitchens	Traditional Ivory	Solid Oak	Lyndale, in-frame
Sun holiday	Package holiday from UK to Spain	Package holiday from UK to Seychelles	Tailored tour with special events
Men's suits	Hugo Boss	Armani	Tom Ford
Ladies' shoes	River Island	Kurt Geiger	Jimmy Choo
Train travel	Regular class		First class
Airline	Economy	Business class	First class
Egg distributor	Regular		Free range/ organic
Milk producer	Private label milk	Branded milk	Fortified with vitamins

Samples, tastings and testers

There was a time when the aisles of supermarket retailers were crowded with promotional people in white coats, bombarding you with samples of sausages or other such tastings. The effect with consumers was immediate, and if the demonstrators were commercially strong, they would 'sell' lots of product. For a number of reasons, it's not done quite so much anymore, but the idea was a good one. Airport retailers still engage you with tastings of Baileys or whiskies and so on. But the masters of this practice are the beauty houses. They have lots of testers on display at their counters for consumers to play with. They will also give away samples with each purchase, because they know it inspires further purchases. If you're not convinced, have a look at the commercial results of the main players in that industry, who have been doing it for years.

Fashion retailers have fitting rooms, motor dealers will offer you a test-drive, and Kara Academy might offer you a free two-hour 'taster' session. Are you likely to buy a pair of sunglasses without trying them on? How many times have you downloaded a 'free' app on your smartphone, to find yourself then targeted by the app developer to buy the full premium version?

What's the equivalent taster opportunity for your business, regardless of whether you're B2C or B2B?

Pack sizes

Pack sizes are influenced by a number of factors: packaging cost savings, delivery cost efficiencies, shelf size, product safety, and picking efficiencies. For example, it takes the same length of time for a warehouse operative to walk to a location and pick up either one or twelve boxes of widgets. If the overall cost for the operative for that single journey is 10c, that 10c split across twelve boxes is a lot lower than it is for picking one. It's simple maths.

An organisation recently did a review of why they were carrying too much stock and discovered that the buyers were buying in bulk to achieve a target intake margin. The buyer was buying too many simply to get a volume discount. The sell-through of the product however, was not fast enough. The financial controller eventually interrogated the process and discovered the problem. The solution was to drop the particular supplier whose pack sizes did not match the rate of sale. Perhaps if the supplier had been asked to reconsider before being dropped, it might have conformed to save the business.

What's right for the customer? When did you last check? Rather than just doing the maths from your own perspective and supply side, consider the implications for your customer.

Best and worst sellers

With modern technology, regardless of levels of sophistication, you should find it easy to identify your best and worst sellers. This makes commercial sense so that you manage your stock levels, your presentation and your marketing accordingly. But this also matters to your customers.

Customers will take comfort and reassurance from your honesty when you tell them that something is a best seller. But be careful – that doesn't mean it's okay to lie and pretend that a 'dog' is a best seller. As a short term response, they might believe you and buy. But if their purchase does not suit their needs, they will be upset with you afterwards.

Of course that doesn't mean that all 'worst sellers' are dogs. Perhaps you haven't promoted or sold them effectively in the past. Just be careful – be customer focused. Your dogs usually end up being sold at a reduced price in your promotions or in your 'SALE'. At least the customer knows this in advance, and there is a level of honesty in that.

This feedback data is important for you. The starting point is to interrogate why a product is a good or bad seller. If you know why it's a great seller, can you sustain it, and for how long? Can you repeat that success with other products?

Similarly, with worst sellers, can you address and correct the reasons why something is not selling? Is it to do with price, quality, colour, size, packaging, positioning or timing?

Know your competition

If you come to work with blinkers on and don't take note of your competitors' activity, you'll be in trouble. It's just good practice to keep an eye on what they are up to. If you don't know for sure, find out. When you do, you will make better informed judgements about your strategy and tactics.

Don't just respond to them in a knee-jerk fashion. Have your strategy formulated, but with due consideration for what others are doing. Using the brand Competitive Positioning Matrix from an earlier chapter, and other models, will help you to determine opportunities for differentiation and not to get caught out!

SUMMARY

In most industries and organisations, customers are initially drawn to your product range, branding, pricing, quality and so on. Depending on where you see yourself on the Competitive Positioning Matrix, you've got to work out your point of differentiation and stick to it. This chapter suggests lots of ways to determine *what good looks like.* When you have figured out your product proposition and what you own by using these guidelines, you've got to make it happen.

Key Takeaways:

- Balance your own needs to make money with the product/service needs of your target customer base
- Consider your ideal positioning in your Competitive Positioning Matrix and develop a product/service offer to match that
- Flagships and category killers will give you opportunities for differentiation and ownership

- Customers do respond positively to exclusivity and newness – these are footfall drivers
- Know your ideal price architecture relevant to your ideal market positioning – what is 'good', what is 'better' and what is 'best'?

Key Questions For You:

- What categories can you dominate and 'own'?
- Does your product range match your aspired position in the competitive marketplace?
- Do you have a sensible range of products or services at varying price levels?

Watch For These Pitfalls:

- If you push your worst sellers on the wrong customer at the wrong time, you're in danger of losing the lifetime value of that customer
- While knee-jerk reactions to competitors are not wise, nor is it safe to arrogantly ignore them
- Pricing is a whole other issue – but be sure to monitor competitor activity for all issues to do with product

Chapter Four

Deliver Premium Through People

What does good look like when it comes to your people? What are the key touchpoints of when they interact and interface with your customer? This section deserves close attention. In many cases where each of the 3 Ps are weighted, *people* regularly comes out as the most important of all. While *product* and *place* are of course important, on their own they will not make a customer feel special. Only a person can do that.

Research on complaints shows more examples to do with *people* than anything else (such as policy, process, product etc.). You yourself will have had experiences of the unhelpful or rude receptionist or salesperson who really annoyed you and caused your blood to boil. In many ways, this whole topic could be made simple by telling your people to treat others as they'd want to be treated themselves, or to do what their parents told them as children and to simply say *please* and *thank you*. While that would indeed be a fantastic start, as leaders we do need more than that.

Knowledge, attitude, skill

Think about what it takes to be great at your job, regardless of your role. People need a sufficient level of *knowledge* to do their jobs. They also need to have a positive *attitude*, and, of course, they need an appropriate set of *skills* to do the job that is expected of them.

To prove the point – take the example of a 24-year-old guy who has had an ambition all of his life to be a pilot. Imagine he buys every book available on the market and acquires all the *knowledge* possible. It's also fair to assume that he probably has a really positive *attitude* to go along with that. Can he now fly a plane? Of course not!

He also needs to develop his *skills* in a flight simulator and get feedback and guidance from his tutor on what he did right and what he might have done wrong.

Picture a person who has been doing a particular job very well for the last twenty years. More than likely, they will have sufficient *knowledge* and *skills* to the job well. But imagine a scenario where they have gone off the boil lately, despite the fact that no new knowledge or skills were required. The chances are that their attitude has changed – possibly to do with some objections to the company, or with boredom, personal life changes, or complacency. The bottom line is that without the right attitude, productivity will be affected.

This is such a simple but effective framework that it also serves as a prompt for creating job descriptions and competency kits. Under each heading, ask yourself: what are the key characteristics required to do the job well?

Knowledge

What do your people need to know in order to do their jobs well? In no particular order, they need knowledge of:

- Company history and heritage, which helps to build a sense of belonging and understanding of the past
- Brand DNA, vision and mission – to provide context for their jobs
- How you differentiate from your competitors – your USPs
- Who is who in the organisation – organisation structure
- What is expected from them and to what standard
- Product mix, price architecture, and USPs
- Supply chain overview
- Product features and benefits – more than your customers can learn from Google searches
- Best and worst sellers
- Actual customers, segmentation, target customer profiles, and geographies
- Key customers by name
- Competitors and what their USPs are – opportunities and threats
- Processes, rules and regulations

What are the risks if your people don't have this knowledge? How will it affect the confidence of your people, their motivation, customer service, sales, efficiencies, complaints and so on? Who is responsible for ensuring your people have this knowledge? Because every organisation has its own set of unique answers to these questions, that makes you responsible.

Attitude

Culture is covered in more detail later in this book. For now, it should be acknowledged that culture has a major effect on the attitudes and subsequent behaviours of your people. A good and positive attitude usually means that people will get on well with each other and that customers will get good service. A bad or negative attitude – well, it's just a pain in the ass to work in that atmosphere. Customers also notice it instantly in how they are treated.

You can train your people on everything that they need to know and do in order to do their jobs well. You may even give them the relevant skills. But if they don't have the right attitude, all the training in the world won't make a difference. A poor attitude permeates the team and it can be like a disease. Others pick up on it and can be infected by it too.

It's true that some individuals are just negative and have a poor attitude to everything that they do. Attitude is a choice that people make, but of course it can be influenced by management, atmosphere, conditions, and other circumstances. If you have attitude issues across the board, then it's time to look at yourself. Ask yourself what is causing it. Whatever the cause, you have to nip it in the bud. Simply transferring the negative person to another department is not the answer.

If it is isolated to certain individuals only, you need to dig deeper to find out why. But keep in mind that many organisations *hire for attitude* and they *train for knowledge and skill.*

I have always been a great believer in Customer Service and at Dubai Duty Free this is one of the cornerstones of our business. We set up our own in-house training department many years ago and all of our employees undergo an induction programme as well as ongoing training by our in-house team or by third party consultants, such as Kara. We currently have 47 nationalities working at Dubai Duty Free, and we believe that this mix of nationalities helps when it comes to interacting with our multi-national customers.

In 2017, our in-house team conducted a total of 968 training sessions with a great deal of emphasis placed on providing a first-class customer service in a bustling environment, which an airport inevitably is. We believe it is important to recognise and reward our staff when they provide outstanding customer service and our 'Gotcha' programme is aimed specifically at identifying and rewarding exceptional customer service. In 2017, there were 9,488 staff observations carried out by the Gotcha team resulting in 70 team stars and 7,929 individual stars awarded.

Our Mobile Customer Service units are also very active and their role is to assist passengers, whether they are shopping or not. Last year the Mobile Customer Service Units directly assisted over 760,000 passengers.

Colm McLoughlin. Executive Vice-Chairman and CEO, Dubai Duty Free

Skill

Skill is defined as the ability to do something well. You as an organisation invest in payroll, and so you deserve for your people to give you the best return on that investment. But you also have a duty to help them develop the relevant skills to do the job in your organisation. You may have been focused in your search and hired a person with a particular set of skills. But are there any differences or nuances that make your process or product different? Keep in mind too that the world is changing constantly, and so is the need to develop new skills.

Hiring a person with specialist skills is one way, but many organisations promote people internally. That of course is a good thing, but here is a regular mistake that organisations make. They take their best salespeople and promote them to be sales managers. On the face of it, that sounds like a reasonable thing to do. It's good for progression, motivation, possible role-modelling and so on. But managing a sales team is an entirely different set of skills to just selling. It may require financial skills, people management skills, strategic thinking, and planning. History is full of stories of failed promotions that could have been avoided with a little more empathy and thought by organisational leaders.

Prioritise skill development – however you do it.

Here again, the retail and hospitality worlds have cracked this, so it makes sense to borrow from their experience. For this example, we'll focus on the skills required for customer-facing people. A great interaction between salesperson and customer is made up of two factors:

- *Process* – the structured steps in the selling cycle (the selling ceremony)
- *Behaviours* – focusing on *how* and *what* our people say and do

Why do you need both? Well, salespeople might follow the selling ceremony *process* to the letter, but if they were to greet customers with grunts or grumpy faces (which is *behaviour*), that is unacceptable.

Here is an overview of the selling ceremony:

Selling Ceremony – Process
1. Appearance
2. Proactive Greeting
3. Establish Needs
4. Present Options
5. Handle Objections
6. Close the Sale
7. Link Sale
8. Farewell Greeting

On the face of it, this looks like a selling model. It is! However, if you accept that every member of your team is selling something at each moment-of-truth, or customer interaction, this model will work almost every time for every customer-facing role.

Let us take each step in turn:

1. Appearance

If the encounter is face to face, the first thing that happens is that the customer sees your team member. The customer initially judges the total effect of the individual, which is mainly about appearance.

Appearance includes being visible and available, with great grooming and good hygiene, an attractive uniform if there is one, positive facial expressions and smiling to show welcome and friendliness. Confident eye contact and body language will show sincerity and readiness to serve.

2. Greeting

A warm, friendly greeting is essential and helps to build rapport and trust. A common excuse is that 'we were busy'. Well, that's not good enough. We should be ever-ready to greet our customers, with:

- Good eye contact and an appropriate salutation, such as *Good morning!*
- Proactive means that you should say hello first. Some organisations have taken this so seriously that they have *meeters and greeters* whose sole purpose is to welcome you as you enter
- A warm *tone of voice* that shows friendliness, interest and sincerity. The tone should be pleasant, friendly and clear

3. Establish needs

Customers have needs, and they don't always express them clearly or indeed even know what their precise needs are. It's the salesperson's job to uncover those needs, so that they can in turn fulfil those needs. The customer's needs might be a tangible product or something less tangible such as information.

Ask the right questions in a conversational way to establish the nature of the customer's needs.

Whatever you are selling will determine the questions to ask. For example, a suit salesperson should ask customers about their preferences for brand, style, cut, colour, size and fit, and when appropriate, their budget. A car salesperson might want to know what purpose the car will be used for (how many kilometres per annum), space requirement, driving style, colour, accessories, other driver's requirements, and budget.

For most products or services, there are likely to be about four or five main chunks of information required to enable you to match your product/service to a customer's needs. Use open-ended questions to get customers talking more freely so as to establish their priorities, likes and dislikes. Open-ended questions include *who, what, where, when, which and how*. Listen carefully to the answers given.

4. *Present options*

The salesperson will present a small number of options (maybe a better one and a best one) to match the information given and give appropriate advice and expertise. Up-sell by showing the options, particularly focusing on how your product can satisfy the needs that the customer expressed earlier.

Customers are more likely to buy when it is clear what your product will do for them. That is why great salespeople focus on the benefits of their product, rather than just the features. For example, imagine you are selling a car and the customer told you that he drives 40,000 kilometres per year. That customer will be more motivated to buy your car if you as the salesperson focus on the running cost of the electric engine, rather than simply saying it's electric!

5. *Handle objections*

The salesperson won't always get it right with the first suggestion, so be prepared for rejection. However, this shouldn't be seen as outright rejection, but simply as an objection to your suggestion. The salesperson should ask for more clarity and then try again.

- *Remember, an objection is not a rejection!*

6. *Close the sale*

Many salespeople struggle with this part of the selling ceremony, perhaps through fear of coming across as pushy, or of rejection. That's such a pity, especially if good rapport has been established and the steps above have been followed closely.

When you know for sure that customers are happy with their selections, gently nudge them along to the closing by getting them to say words such as: *'Okay, I'll go with that then!'*

7. *Link sale*

Before parting company or actually taking the customer's cash or payment details, there is an opportunity to add further satisfaction for both the customer and your organisation.

- Offer a complementary item to go with the main purchase. If done effectively, this can come across as great service (you've just thought of something that's in the customer's interest) more than trying to get more money from them.
- Propose a linked item very gently. For example, say: *'Just so you know, we also have fabulous ties to complement that shirt.'*
- The value to the organisation is of course, increased sales.
- Again, link selling is not just about product – a receptionist might ask: *'Is there anything else I can do for you today?'*

8. Farewell greeting

It might be tempting at this point to just take the money and run! But remember the first chapter's reference to *lifetime value*, where you want to treat customers so well that they will come back again? At this final stage of the interaction, do your best to show appreciation. Thank customers and make them feel special. Reassure them on their choices and give some added piece of advice or best wishes, or whatever is warm and friendly.

We've made the point that this process is extremely effective in the retail and hospitality sectors. Now apply it to every person in your organisation that interacts with customers. Is there really any difference? Not everyone is selling a tangible product or service. Take a receptionist for example. The product that he or she is 'selling' is information. The same steps above will work here too. A truck driver may not have as much to say in step 3 above, which is to *establish needs*, but using all the other steps would be professional and appropriate.

If it's a contact centre interaction on the telephone, where the customer cannot see your person (*Appearance*), then what is the alternative? It has to be tone of voice more than anything... then continue with steps 2-8 above.

> *In a world of seemingly endless technological disruption, it may ironically turn out that people are the biggest competitive advantage of all. Retail overwhelmingly remains human-to-human. The best retailers know that since their salespeople are the walking ambassadors for a brand. Only companies with engaged, empowered, and passionate employees will thrive and survive.*
>
> Blaine Callard, CEO Harvey Norman Ireland

What behaviours are appropriate?

Remember, process on its own is not enough. Along with the eight steps of the Selling Ceremony, we should be conscious of *how* we do the various steps. That's what we mean by *behaviours*. Think through what the appropriate behaviours are for your organisation – based on who you are as a company (brand DNA) and expectations in your industry. But you're unlikely to go wrong by again by following retail and hospitality here:

Courtesy

At the time of writing, Google presented this definition:

- *The showing of politeness in one's attitude and behaviour toward others*
- *A polite speech or action, especially one required by convention*

As before – it's using the *please* and *thank you* that you learned as a child. Be nice and ensure a pleasant tone of voice.

Efficiency

Google: *Performing or functioning in the best possible manner with the least waste of time and effort.*

Most customers are under pressure for time and they don't need that pressure added to by un-necessary delays. Make sure you show a sense of urgency. As for queues, ensure that the process is respectful of the customers' time and the money they are spending with you. If you're a contact centre, be careful of leaving the caller waiting too long.

Finesse

Google: *Do (something) in a subtle and delicate manner.*

Regardless of where you sit in the competitive marketplace, it is never okay to be gruff or sloppy with your customers. Even if you position yourself low on price, it's never okay to be rude, dismissive, or rough with your customers.

All three behaviours above are important and are deliberately shown in this sequence. For example, if you skipped *courtesy* and behaved rudely toward a customer, yet were *efficient* and had *finesse*, the customer wouldn't be impressed. In fact, *courtesy* almost acts like a buffer. You just might get away with a lack of *efficiency* or *finesse* if you are very *courteous* throughout. Of course, that is not a recommendation to not concern yourself with all three.

Between getting the behaviours right and the eight steps in the selling ceremony, you might think that this is over-complicated for a receptionist, telephonist, delivery driver, engineer or any other representative of your organisation. But before you dismiss it, think of who these people are interacting with daily. Then think about the total impact of your employees' behaviour on your future business potential. Don't dismiss – just edit it accordingly.

The three behaviours here should merge with the *selling ceremony* where appropriate. For example:

Selling Ceremony – Process	Behaviour – Examples Only
Appearance	Finesse
Proactive Greeting	Courtesy, Efficiency and Finesse
Establish Needs	Courtesy
Present Options	Efficiency
Handle Objections	Courtesy and Finesse
Close the Sale	Efficiency
Link Sale	Courtesy and Finesse
Farewell Greeting	Courtesy, Efficiency and Finesse

3 Cs!

The eight steps above work every time in almost all customer-facing situations. But if you're concerned that there is a little too much detail here, consider this short edited version: *Connect, Consult, Conclude.*

Picture a team of stewards at a concert, in a busy airport, or at a busy shopping centre. You as the organiser or landlord may want to create a good impression of friendliness and professionalism. At the very least, your stewards should know how to greet people, offer help proactively and make customers feel special. Try this simple tool and train your people on these basics:

- ***Connect:*** Smile and say hello
- ***Consult:*** Engage with the customers and offer help
- ***Conclude:*** Thank the customers and wish them good day

This is a tool that might be used as a simple framework and prompt for great service, but it's more than that. If this simple CCC is set as the expected norm of your people, that will also act as a stimulus and constant reminder of the new culture that you are developing. It will be a fundamental basic platform for you to build on later.

Meeters and greeters

> *Neither Sam nor I had ever seen such a thing so we started talking to him. He explained that he had a dual purpose: to make people feel good about coming in, and to make sure people weren't walking back out the entrance with merchandise they hadn't paid for.*
>
> Tom Coughlin, Wal-Mart, in conversation with Sam Walton when on a visit to one of their own stores that had a Meeter and Greeter

It's funny... sometimes an idea that was thought up for one purpose can then fulfil another need. The main message here, though, is about making visitors and customers feel good. While it may be a bit extravagant for you to have greeters in your business, the message and intent is still the same. We should be humbled each and every time a customer chooses to make contact with us, and treat them accordingly. Eye contact, a hello and a smile will go a long way.

SUMMARY

In our 3-legged stool framework (Product, People, Place), many would say that *People* is more important than the other two. That is very often true, but it can vary from industry to industry. *Product* and *Place* are of course important, but on their own they will not make a customer feel special. Only a person can do that.

SUMMARY

To do any job well, we all need to have a combination of *knowledge, attitude* and *skill*. Your customers judge you daily based on their interactions with your people. Ensure that your employees have the appropriate KAS (knowledge, attitude and skill), which should reflect your desired position in the competitive matrix.

Key Takeaways:

- Know the profile of your ideal employee, in terms of knowledge, attitude and skills
- Getting the right people starts with recruitment
- A great greeting is the best start to most human interactions
- If you are truly customer focused, you'll listen more than tell, and you'll adapt accordingly
- The right person will know the steps in giving great service (eight steps) but will also know the right behaviours every time
- Basic courtesy will cover up weaknesses in selling skills – customers are more likely to go along with and buy from a nice person than a rude person who knows how to sell

Key Questions For You:

- Have you thought about how you want your customers to be treated by your own people?
- Have you defined the competencies for each role using knowledge, attitude and skills – to match your expectation and brand?
- Have you communicated your standards to all your people, both new and existing?
- Have you trained them on how to interact or sell to your customers, in line with your desired brand positioning?

Watch For These Pitfalls:

- Employees may well know the selling process outlined above – but if they are grumpy or rude, they'll misrepresent your brand
- The selling ceremony (process) on its own is not enough, as it is possible to follow the steps and to be rude at the same time

DELIVER PREMIUM THROUGH PLACE

Imagine you are inviting friends or family around to your home for dinner. What impression do you want to make? Would you be happy for them to see your home like a pigsty? Of course not, because your pride and dignity would not allow it. You'd much prefer to show them respect, and that they see a clean, tidy and well presented home that you are proud of. Why then, do some businesses so often allow their housekeeping standards to be so poor? Isn't your business (or your part of the business) just an extension of yourself? What impression does it leave with your visitors if your location is dirty, dishevelled, or hard to access or navigate?

Place – What does good look like?

Place as a topic is very extensive, and it can mean different things depending on your business model. For simplicity here, let's split the whole of industry like this:

- *Your place* – this is when a customer comes to your premises, such as if you are a restaurant, hotel, retailer, motor dealer, bank (outer and inner offices), government department, hospital, clinic, solicitor's office, etc. In these cases, *Place* is everything to do with the physical environment.
- *Customer's place* – this is where you are delivering your physical or digital goods to your customer's premises, such as if you are a manufacturer, distributor, wholesaler, tradesman, consultant, developer, etc. Here, *place* is more about your *route to market*.

We'll now deal with them separately for the rest of this section. As a reminder, don't forget that *what good looks like* for your business should be determined by who you aspire to be as a brand and your competitive positioning. (See the Competitive Positioning Matrix in Chapter 2.) The various sub-headings to follow will prompt you for what is important. The answers to those questions should be determined by who you want to be as a brand and where you aspire to be in that matrix.

Do not skip this section just because you are not a retailer or hotel! The lessons here can be applied to all businesses.

Your place

The first part of this chapter is for your business if customers come to your premises.

Access

Imagine you are at home and set off on a trip to your local supermarket which is situated on its own site. You will judge the *place* from when you arrive, starting perhaps with the car park. Some shopping malls use a number sequence and others use a colour system. Whatever you do, make sure that your customers can easily find their cars on their return. The Brown Thomas car park in Dublin is quite unique in that it has several entry and exit points. The spaces are wider than usual and the turning circles on each ramp are wide enough for SUV type cars. In addition to its proximity to a great store, the added extras of this car park are a big plus under *place*.

When Disneyland guests arrive early in the morning, full of excitement and anticipation with their families, they regularly forget where they left their cars. At exit time, if a guest seems to be struggling to find a car, a steward will simply ask them what approximate time they arrived and then show them to the area where it's most likely that they parked. How do they do it? Disney use a time of arrival system, where Disney stewards log and track where cars parked during blocks of time. Remember too that Disney guests are likely to arrive for a full day of entertainment, so in fairness it is easy for them.

Whether you directly control the car park or not, you should influence it, as it is part of the customer experience. Even if you are a business in a town centre, be mindful of the level of effort that customers have to expend to get to you, find a trolley and return to their cars. If there is a charge for parking near your premises, why not have some loose change available to make it easier for your customers? If there is a parking app for your locality, why not teach customers how to use it?

The entrance doorway and reception of your premises should be clear and uncluttered, welcoming and easy to access. Once your customers enter, they encounter all sorts of messages. Let's start with housekeeping.

Housekeeping, hygiene standards and health and safety

On a recent visit to the head office of a top food manufacturer, it was noted that the reception area was cluttered and dirty, with lots of boxes sitting on the counter and out of date newspapers. The bin was overflowing, and some slats of the window blinds were twisted. The floor had a series of books a mobile book vendor had placed there, hoping that staff and visitors would buy some. The television was placed oddly and awkwardly on the wall behind the receptionist. It seemed to have been positioned closest to the plug socket, rather than with consideration for balance, aesthetics or sightlines – or indeed, the viewers.

What does all this say about that company? Do they care about detail and what perceptions they create in the minds of their visiting customers? Leadership guru Rene Carayol often talks about how he can read and tell a lot about the culture of an organisation by observing what goes on in reception. (In fairness, that is not just about *place*; it's also about the *people* and their behaviours.)

How would you feel if you arrive to a store and the aisles are cluttered or too narrow for you and your child's buggy, or the floors, ceiling or walls are dirty? What impression do you get if the carpet in your local pub is sticky? You suddenly wonder what else is hidden by the toned-down lighting.

A high profile DIY chain has designed their stores with a public toilet in the foyer. Although it's a customer convenience, the entrance is not the best place to put it. Worse, on several visits it was neither working properly nor clean, not to mention the smell. It would be better placed down at the back of the store. Another example was a lawyer's office with a display of dead flowers in the window. The brasses were filthy and there were dirty outdoor boots just inside the door on full view. The boots were obviously conveniently placed for the lawyer for going on site visits to building sites or farms. Now the boots had to go somewhere, but did they really have to be on view to the public?

Here is an issue with banks and the manager's inner office! It's understandable that in a private working office, one might have family pictures, a messy desk, spare shoes on the floor, files piled high, etc. But a customer going from the main branch area into a manager's office to discuss financial affairs is similar to a customer in a department store moving from one department to another. Wouldn't it send a very mixed message if you experienced a pristine environment in the fragrance hall of a department store, and then found a total mess in the shoe department? Banks have 'departments' too and should convey similar and consistent messages throughout the branch.

On a recent visit to a bank manager, a customer was brought in to the manager's small office. There was one chair for the manager on her side of the desk, and two chairs on the opposite side for the customer. However, it was impossible for the customer's knees to fit under the desk, due to the presence of a modesty screen! Consequently, the customer had to sit back and sideways from the desk, which created a gap and awkwardness when it came to signing documents. Obviously the desks were designed by the 'politically correct department' and no member of the bank had tried the seating out from the customer's perspective beforehand.

Remember that customers are intent on spending money with you, so treat them with the respect that they deserve. Now you may say that 'we can't all be Four Seasons Hotel' and so on. Well, that is true, because what you get in Four Seasons is way beyond the basic housekeeping standards. The challenge back to you is: whatever business you are in and wherever you aspire to be in your competitive matrix – is it ever okay to have poor standards? This is not always about money. It's often more about recognising the importance of housekeeping in the first place, setting a standard and sticking to it.

Step outside and walk back into your own premises with the mind of a customer. What do you see? What would you change?

Merchandising standards

In retail, visual merchandising is the manipulation of attractive displays, merchandising and floor plans to engage customers and boost sales. Merchandising is about presenting your product in its best possible way to appeal to the customer. This might be a physical product on a shop floor, a set of brochures on an exhibition stand or the credentials presenter in the hand of an estate agent or consultant. In all cases, think about structure, standards and visual appeal.

If you are a retailer, you already know the basic rules of merchandising. The purpose of merchandising is to make the product visually appealing and easy for the customer to buy. Key elements and examples include:

- Everything clean and tidy
- Neat displays, balanced and symmetrical
- Products – front faced out
- Correct signage and ticketing – and in the right place
- Colour co-ordinated
- In size and/or price order – facing the same direction

Many hotels now make an effort to attract guests to their fine dining restaurants by dressing a table outside the door of the restaurant, inside the lobby area. They don't show real food, but they will often show well photographed illustrations. In the carvery restaurant of the Radisson Blu Hotel at Dublin Airport, the chefs make a big effort to make their area more attractive with creative displays of exotic foods to be seen by customers while queuing. They will often have some fun or theatre in their display, which can bring on a smile.

> *We in the Gleneagle Hotel Group have always been passionate about customer service. We try very hard to provide real hospitality and a great Irish welcome to our guests from all over the world. As customers' expectations keep changing, I believe that complacency is the enemy of innovation so we challenge ourselves consistently to improve even more.*
>
> Patrick O'Donoghue, CEO, The Gleneagle Hotel Group

Pubs might take some of this on board. How often do you approach a bar and see empty glasses on the back shelf facing you, the customer, in your line of sight? While that might be functionally efficient for the bar staff, it does nothing for the opportunity to entice the customer or for the bar staff to up-sell. Empty glasses would be better placed under the counter out of sight, leaving shelves that are visible to customers for promoting brands or house specials. That's maximising your real estate.

> *In the hospitality sector, and the pub sector in particular, customer expectations now centre around the total experience. Whether it be drink alone or a combination of food and drink the demands are greater. Good food and quality drinks are prerequisites but insufficient on their own. There must be a range of drinks to suit all tastes, it must be served in appropriate glassware and, in many cases, with a level of theatre in the serving.*
>
> *Apart from demanding consistent quality, patrons now need to know the sources of food, how local it is and want it served with a smile. You need to be able to tell the story behind the product. To compliment all of that the ambience needs to be appealing, be modern without being flash and toilets must be top grade. To be successful both now and in the future an operator must combine all of the above and more.*
>
> Padraig Cribben, CEO, Vintners Federation of Ireland (VFI)

In the world of beauty and skin care, the power of brands is very strong. Those brands often dictate to retailers how they should merchandise their goods. They have lots of science and market research at their disposal. They have mastered the concept of category management to the point that they know exactly how their products sell best. However, this vertical and almost selfish approach does not always work for the consumer. For example, on a recent trip through a European airport, a male customer wanted to buy men's fragrance. That proved difficult as all fragrances were merchandised within their respective brands – women's and men's all together. Women may be very loyal to beauty brands and quite happy to see products displayed by brand. Men would much rather see all men's fragrances together and women's separately. The best answer to suit all in this case is to dual-site the men's fragrance!

Signage

In his amazing book *Why We Buy*, Paco Underhill talks about a successful gas filling station in the US with a high number of female customers. Part of the reason for its success is due to a giant sign declaring: *We have the cleanest toilets for 50 miles.* Unsurprisingly, they happen to have a very high percentage of female customers. Signage can be very powerful, so long as it is concise, easy to read and relevant. There is a great pub in London City with a huge sign proclaiming: *We have the best fish and chips in London*. That is obviously a very subjective statement and hard to prove, but it does express the confidence they have in their own product. Good for them.

Retail banks have a lot to improve upon here too. With respect to banks, the products they sell are not tangible. They have to rely on signage, slogans, brochures and pictures. Such collateral should, of course, be placed appropriately in line with the customer flow. Consider this: most customers entering a retail branch are more focused on their primary transactions and reasons for entering in the first place. How likely are they to absorb messages about credit cards or home or car loans on the way in? Yet banks typically direct most of their signage out towards the door to the incoming customer. Wouldn't it be appropriate if even some of the signage also faced back into the branch, to be observed by customers when they are finished with their transactions and exiting the premises?

There are three tiers of hierarchy for signage:

1. *Navigational* – to help you move around a large space such as a theme park, department store or hotel
2. *Category* – to clearly identify product categories, for example, to separate laptop computers or smartphones (multi-feature versus basic)
3. *Product signage* – to explain the product specifications/history to the browser

What does all this mean for non-retailers? It shows how tidiness, visual appeal and attention to detail can make life more pleasant for your customers.

Adjacencies in retail

When you go to do your weekly grocery shopping, you are unlikely to find the detergents on the same shelf as the bread! Apart from the health and safety issue, it just doesn't make sense. Why? To answer this, you have to get inside the minds of the shoppers and their shopping journey. The notion of adjacencies applies at macro level, such as how categories are arranged in the masterplan floor layout. At a micro level, it includes what brands or products go where *within* a category.

At a micro level, the issue of which brand of cheese is at eye level and which is not is usually determined by the category management planogram. Margin and best or worst sellers all feed into that decision.

However, at a macro level, careful consideration should also be given to category adjacencies. With tongue in cheek, Paco Underhill would recommend that men's gadgets might be placed beside the lingerie department in a big store. His point is that the men would be occupied while the women shop in peace. While this may not be very visually appealing, you can see his point.

A department store in Germany seems to adapt that advice to their floor layout. On the ground floor, which houses the Ladies Accessories, Beauty and Fragrance departments, they have men's socks in the corner. Given that 99% of the shoppers on the ground floor are female, this just doesn't make sense – scientifically, visually or commercially. Customers have perceptions of natural category groupings. You've only got to get into the minds of the shoppers and their shopping plans and journey to get it right.

Non-retailers can learn from this too. Find cross-selling opportunities in whatever way you can, such as your brochures, correspondence and other collateral.

Ambience and senses

The science of shopping has become very sophisticated. Today we know so much more about how customers buy. We know for example that customers are often influenced more by emotional (heart) issues than practical (head) issues. The use of senses, sight, sound, touch, smell and taste, can affect that. Great authors of novels know this too. When telling their stories, they will often try to transport the reader to another place by describing the scene through the senses. Consider:

- *Sight*: Products should be visually appealing in terms of how they are presented.
- *Sound*: If there is music, it should be age appropriate and not overbearing. Music too can help to create strong memories. This also applies to 'hold' music on a telephone. Is *Greensleeves* played by digital sounds really appropriate?
- *Touch*: This allows the customers to experience the product in the hand, in the fitting room, and so on
- *Smell*: This is often described as the most important sense, as it stimulates the emotions more than the others. The Marriott Hotel Group have a particular 'Marriott scent' that you will find in almost every Marriott hotel around the world.
- *Taste*: This is instant, and customers will either like or not like your product.

Theatre

Theatre is a concept that has garnered more prominence these days in terms of how it can influence a customer's experience. Static, boring displays do nothing to stimulate a purchase. When theatre is introduced it can serve to entertain, to romance and ultimately to sell product. Theatre can come in many forms, such as movement, colour, fun, novelty, education, edutainment (something educational that is also entertaining), and intertainment (where the customer is invited to interact with something). Theatre has to be brand relevant at the same time.

Theatre is powerful if it captures the imagination of the customer. It should interrupt the mundane and of course, should not be boring.

Theatre is not just for hotels and retailers. It can also apply to an office environment, a reception area, a PowerPoint presentation, a brochure, etc. When presented effectively, it can give great support to a brand.

Effort

In this time-poor world we live in, customers will punish you if they have to apply more effort than is reasonable to buy from you. That might apply to the waiting time on a call, the queuing time in a bank, the difficulty in getting to your premises, parking challenges, public transport constraints, on-line purchases, return policy and so on.

Take time to walk through the journey just as your customer would to establish the pain points.

Wi-fi

One of the first things that people do when they arrive to a new place, destination or venue is to check for wi-fi. 'Always-connected' is a new reality in their lives, and businesses might ignore this at their peril. Customers might leave to go to a place where they can log on. Similarly, if they have to pay for wi-fi access, they'll leave and go somewhere where they can get it for free. This doesn't just apply to young people, of course; people of all ages may expect that. Some departments store retailers find this to be quite an expensive and practical challenge if they have multiple floors and a high volume of footfall. Nevertheless, it's a new standard that has to be embraced by all businesses.

Digital payments

There was a time recently when restaurants that didn't have a portable credit-card machine to accommodate payment at the table were seen to be out of touch. Now that contactless payments and payments by smartphone are widely accepted, B2C businesses have a new challenge. Rather than seeing this as a cost, however, see it as an investment.

If you partner with the right payments provider, you can have access to amazing basket-level data about your customers' buying habits and preferences. Yoyo is one such UK based company. Their app (which can be tailored for any company) offers a combination of loyalty tracking and payments. With the loyalty element, they can track any one customer and enable the business to market specific promotion to individuals, based on their preferences and habits. This maximises the marketing spend as it focuses your promotion on those most likely to avail of it. The alternative 'old' method is to place an ad on television or radio or in print, all of which have a lower success rate.

Customer's place – your route to market

If your organisation is a type that takes your product to the customer, such as a distributor, manufacturer, tradesman, consultant or estate agent, then *place* is more about your route to market and how well that represents your brand.

Order process

Let's start with the order process itself. How efficient is that for your customers? Do you offer choice that suits your customers, such as on-line ordering, telephone or face-to-face? Finding the balance between efficiency, accuracy and personal touch is an ongoing challenge. What's right for both your customers and you?

A wholesaler that sells drinks to the pub trade has a system where they proactively call customers on a given day in a certain window of time. The customer is 'trained' to be ready for the call and have the stock levels checked in advance. Publicans are busy people and are happy to have the wholesaler do the work, so few of them will actually proactively make the call themselves. Not only that, this wholesaler has a competitor who is also vying for the business, so they can better control the order this way. In a customer feedback survey, this wholesaler scored 97% for their order process. That example is obviously very low-tech and they do have other options too, such as on-line ordering. The point is that they flex their system to suit each customer.

Deliveries

While working with a hotel recently, low morale was discovered, particularly in the housekeeping department. It turned out that the housekeeping team were getting their knuckles rapped daily for not having the bedrooms ready on time. On further checking, it turned out that the fresh linen was not being delivered until 3 pm each day! You might argue that management should have known about this and fixed it. Well, they didn't, and that's beside the point in this context. It shows the effect of deliveries on the efficient running of a business. The housekeeping team in this hotel had developed a bad impression of the linen supplier. Of course, once the issue was explained to the linen provider, they changed the schedule immediately to suit the client.

Other concerns with deliveries are to do with the delivery person. Many organisations miss this as a key role in the business. In some cases, the only person that a customer meets on a regular basis is the delivery person. If that person is employed by the company, they should be trained on customer service and their role in delivering great experiences. Grooming, tone, language and behaviour all have an effect. If you outsource the service as many do, you should agree an SLA (service level agreement) with the outsource provider to ensure that *your* customers get an experience that reflects your brand. (More on *people* in the next chapter).

Who pays for your deliveries? This is an ongoing opportunity for negotiation. A recent example of a small organisation supplying quality fish to premium hotels highlighted a big issue here. For years, the supplier was delivering small quantities with no delivery charge. However, it was costing the supplier a fortune. The hotels were enjoying the super service, of course. But once the issue was explained to them, they were quite reasonable and agreed to order larger quantities and less frequently. This didn't cause a problem for them, but it halved the distribution costs for the supplier. Transparency, honesty and dialogue usually wins.

> *In recent times there has been much about 'convergence' in technology. Unfortunately a side effect has been convergence in business offerings too. The latter part of my business life was spent in wholesaling beverages where product differentiation was difficult. What made a significant difference to us as a supplier that our customers valued was the work we did to listen to customers and then to streamline our whole approach to customer service.*
>
> Des Drumm (Retired), Ex Managing Director C&C Wholesale (Now Britvic)

Professionals, such as estate agents, accountants, consultants, etc.

As a professional, you don't have a physical product to show your customer. Therefore, much depends on your own personal presence and the collateral you bring with you. Keep in mind too that your car says a lot about you. That's not to say that you need to have a top of the range premium car. It's more about the cleanliness and what message that sends out.

> *The Institute of Professional Auctioneers and Valuers (IPAV) is an institute made up of a lot of smaller independent members, who look to their Institute for training, education and expert help. In any membership organisation it's very important for members to receive the service help and know how they need to work on a day to day basis. We got across the message of how exceptional service can make you the best whether you are the largest or the smallest fish in the pond. Our membership have benefited tremendously from this passion for customer service.*
>
> Pat Davitt, CEO IPAV

You also might give some consideration to your collateral. You should have a brochure and a business card to leave behind you after you've gone. In the meeting itself, consider having an iPad or a paper version of a presentation that might follow a sensible flow. Consider this example for an estate agent who visits a potential vendor of a residential property, hoping to get the instruction:

- Who we are: heritage, track record
- Specialties (e.g. residential, commercial, agricultural, or whatever is appropriate to this vendor)
- Market knowledge of this segment in this area
- Marketing pack, which includes sample brochures, advertisements, signboards, on-line, office
- Approach when meeting viewers, such as respect, punctuality, info on local schools, etc.
- Valuation and rationale for that
- Sample checklist for seller and buyer to improve efficiency
- Database of existing potential buyers
- A case study
- Fee structure

This is not meant to be a long-winded presentation. Picture the estate agent sitting down over the dining room table after walking around the property. The flow above will help to build confidence in a very competitive marketplace and will help to justify a higher fee structure too.

> *Our DNA is as a consumer company – for that individual customer who's voting thumbs up or thumbs down. That's who we think about. And we think that our job*

is to take responsibility for the complete user experience. And if it's not up to par, it's our fault, plain and simply.

Steve Jobs

SUMMARY

Regardless of whether customers come to your premises or you bring your services to your customers, *place* deserves to reflect where you aspire to be. Far too many organisations downplay the effect of this leg of the stool on the overall experience. Let's agree again that the legs are not necessarily equal in weighting. *People* is usually more important than the other two. But that doesn't mean that it's okay to forget about *place*.

This chapter includes a checklist of key things to discover, regardless of whether you are B2C (customers come to your premises)... B2B (you deliver to the customer)... or a professional service provider.

Key Takeaways:

Your place:

- Check your standards
- It's never okay to have poor standards, regardless of where you aspire to be in the Competitive Positioning Matrix
- Recognise that customers are influenced by the human senses, so exploit them positively to enhance their experience
- Your place is a selling environment, so think like a customer
- Digital is changing the landscape exponentially, so stay up to date and know what's changing

Customer's place, your route to market:

- If you are a wholesaler delivering to customers, check your order process, deliveries, scheduling, paperwork and other collateral
- If you outsource your deliveries, agree on an SLA with your partner
- If you are a professional selling a service, consider a presentation that is visually appealing and tells a great story

Key Questions For You:

- Is *place* even on your radar?
- Does your *place* reflect your brand DNA?
- Do you know what elements of your *place* are important to your customers?
- What is best practice in your sector?

SUMMARY

Watch For These Pitfalls:

- Operational challenges can cause standards to slip (such as broken AC, lights etc.) but don't let that become an excuse for bad standards
- Great standards don't always have to require capital investment
- If you outsource some services such as deliveries or fitting to a third party, be careful that they are not letting you down

Chapter Six

Deliver Premium On-Line

The advances in technology in the last fifty years are quite amazing. In fact, the changes in the last five years are spectacular. But these changes will reduce in significance in the future as change grows exponentially. Gordon Moore (one of the founders of Intel in the 60s) predicted back then that the capacity of a chip would double every two years. That means that, for example, the processors, mainframes and memory banks that would have required the space of a football stadium then can now fit on your desk, or indeed in the cloud! A whole new world has spun out of this technology that has enabled great processing power and even faster growth. This has caused all sorts of disruption for businesses across all industries.

It's hard to believe that there was a time when the only way you could keep up to date with the news was through television, radio and the press. Look at what has happened in the book publishing world, the music industry, TV, travel industry, and retail in general. The list goes on and on. It's also hard to believe that the only way you could have regular contact with loved ones in other parts of the world was through a dial-up telephone or posted letter.

For retailers in particular, the number of touchpoints where the customer can interact with you has exploded. All the touchpoints in traditional 'bricks and mortar' retailing are well known. They include advertisement campaigns, window displays, internal displays, signage, TVs in store, salespeople, delivery people, and so on.

Today, your competitors probably have the same technology as you and can conduct transactions just like you. While technology is important, it is not just about technology any more. It is about your attitude, empathy and honesty when things go wrong, and they do! The customer has to know that you truly care for them and

that you will be there for them when they need you. It may be a time consuming effort but it will bear fruit in terms of prolonged customer contracts and satisfaction.
Goran Abramovic, Ex-European Sales Director, TouchCorp

In the past, Wal-Mart bet on location and an edited inventory list. Of all the digital camera options in the world, they may have listed, say, 30 in their stocklist. By comparison, a pureplay retailer like Amazon probably has 200 different digital cameras. Amazon, in contrast, bet on diversity of products. They did it because they could. After all, they don't have to carry stock of each item.

The concept of omni-channel retailing emerged, where a unification of all sales channels on a single interface around the customer evolved. Macy's bet on omni-channel and grew the business 'around' the customer.

We still have all the traditional channels mentioned earlier, coupled with all the social media platforms (Facebook, Snapchat, Instagram, Google, YouTube, Twitter, etc). Add the website to the mix for browsing, buying and returning goods. Then of course, there are review sites where customers like to leave comments, good and bad. Don't forget the mobile smartphone and how that has changed the world.

But do you see the similarity between the old and new? While there are now a multitude of touchpoints, the fundamental model that drives sales has not changed.

What has not changed?

Here is a basic model that reflects the key drivers of sales, regardless of the platform.

F/F x Conv x ATV = Sales

'F/F' is footfall (called prospects in other industries). If you own a boutique and you manage to get customers to enter your store, you also know that they won't all buy something from you. Browsing is a natural and normal customer behaviour. Your challenge as a business is to convert as many browsers into paying customers as possible. That's 'Conv' in the model above. You'll also have data that tells you the average transaction value ('ATV'), and when you multiply all factors together, that gives you your sales number.

For example, 1,000 x 40% x 50 = 20,000 means that in a given timeframe, you had 1,000 browsing customers or prospects. You converted 40% of them, and on average, they each spent 50 (euros, pounds, dollars, or whatever your currency). All that multiplied together produced a sales figure of 20,000. Let's take this a stage further. Imagine if your footfall or prospects number was 900. If the other factors stayed the same as the above example, your sales total is 18,000.

Sales is a numbers game. From Biblical times to today's world filled with technology options, the fundamentals of business haven't changed. It's really important to not forget that. It's easy to be distracted and confused with all the latest bells and whistles. That puts you at risk of losing sight of what matters.

The options and preferences for what drives footfall or prospects may have changed, but which ones are right for your business? Likewise, the options and preferences for how to convert browsers and increase ATV have also multiplied, but which ones are right for you?

It would be impossible to list all the changes in technology here in this publication. It would be even more ridiculous to anticipate what changes are coming down the line. To do that would put this book out of date in about 24 hours! The intent here is to illustrate that despite all the changes to date and to come, the challenge is coping with it all. You just have to stay close to it. You have to embrace this change to remain relevant.

If children enter an old-fashioned sweet shop and see the shelves lined with an array of tasty, colourful and attractive collections – well, they can't have them all. As a business, you too have to carefully edit what is out there and think strategically about what is right for you. Your budget won't stretch to all the options, and maybe that's a good thing. See technology as an enabler for something, rather than an end in itself. You need a website, but for what? You want to embrace social media, but with what tone of voice and targeted at whom? You want funds to develop an e-commerce platform, but what's the payback? You want to do all of the above? But where is the thread that binds them altogether?

The message here is more about being careful and strategic and to plan ahead. Being reactive and jumping on a band-wagon is a risk to your brand integrity and your P+L. The other big message is to be joined up in your thinking and your strategies. If you're a traditional business (pre-digital), you may be tempted to simply 'bolt on' a digital offering, but that's not how customers see you anymore. Your messaging and routes to market need to be totally joined up so that your customers get a seamless experience across all platforms. Your product suite needs to be the same. Your customer database and your marketing messages need to be consistent. That's the holy grail for all industries today, and that's your challenge too.

Customer changes

Erik Qualman is the founder and CEO of Socialnomics.net. He and his team keep their fingers on the pulse of what's happening in the marketplace, particularly in terms of how people and consumers are changing. Here are some of their examples:

- 50% of the world's population is under 30
- The numbers of people using social platforms keep growing exponentially
- 53% of Millennials would rather lose their sense of smell than their technology
- 93% of buying decisions are influenced by social media
- What happens in Las Vegas no longer stays in Vegas; it stays on YouTube!
- Video accounts for more than two-thirds of mobile usage
- The attention span of a goldfish is eight seconds; for humans it's reduced to seven seconds
- More people own a mobile device than a toothbrush

- One in three marriages start on-line
- The fastest growing demographic on Twitter is grandparents
- Every second, two new people join LinkedIn
- LinkedIn have lowered the age for users to 13

What does all this mean for businesses today? The statistics shown here will constantly change over time and depending on where the research is conducted. But for now, accept them as a realistic indication of how the old world (pre-digital) has changed forever. How you respond and cope is your new challenge.

Let's first explore how to give a great experience on-line in terms of your marketing. This is where you will drive footfall or prospects. Customers now have so many channels available to them that they are always connected, and they are more empowered than ever before.

> *In a world where time is our customer's most valuable asset, customer experience is the measure of whether the time spent interacting with your product or service was worth it from each customer's perspective.*
>
> *Digital has brought about new challenges and opportunities for us all. In the B2B sector, we firmly believe that digital enhances our existing channels – enhancing our customers' experience, by ensuring convenience when a customer wants and needs it.*
>
> Geraldine Moloney, SME Customer Strategy at Electric Ireland

Marketing on-line

Most likely, your products or services are not for everybody, but for a particular segment of the population. How do you find them and communicate with them? In the early days of mass marketing, campaigns were all planned around demographics, such as gender, age, marital status, education and location. Once the campaign was designed, tested and launched, there was no going back. TV and press space was secured, and to change that quickly and cost-effectively was almost impossible.

Where should you go if you want to market your product or service? You go to where people meet and interact. As the Internet developed, the approach to demographic marketing changed completely. Big Data now allows us to target customers based on their behaviours, rather than just demographics. The demographic breakdown has not disappeared (marketing women's clothes to men, for example, is obviously a waste of money). Knowing their behaviours and preferences is so much more accurate. If you are Amazon and you know that a person that bought the 'Jack Reacher' novels by Lee Child also browsed books by Vince Flynn, you can build a behavioural analysis of that customer. If you are Café Nero and you know that a particular customer only ever buys a Flat White on the way to work, perhaps you could target that person with a promotional offer of a croissant.

This personalised approach is both expected by the customer and made possible through technology. Do you ever wonder why certain ads appear on your Google, YouTube or Facebook feeds? The technology in the background is monitoring your behaviour and preferences and building up a profile on you. Some ads work better than others. But Google are so convinced of this as an effective marketing tool that they only charge advertisers for 'click throughs' rather than just impressions. (An 'impression' is where your ad appears on a feed, but may not be clicked).

Here are some steps to take in getting your social presence right and to give a great experience on-line.

1. Research by observing first. Use the various social platforms to research how people interact and what your customers' preferences are.
2. Who are the influencers? Some people have more influence than others. Get close to them and perhaps develop relationships with them. Show them your products and share content with them.
3. Focus on building connections rather than building followers. It doesn't matter if you have 100 or 1,000 friends. It's better to have fewer, engaged fans than many fans that do not relate to your brand or product. It is more important to have strong connections.
4. Give value, not sales pitches. Don't annoy your circle with regular product sales. Share content instead. Videos that educate or entertain on your subject are much more likely to win appeal.
5. Be patient and consistent. Building a social presence takes time, so don't expect immediate results.

> *Entire business models have been created on the back of the staggering power and reach of digital marketing. However customers will be lost as quickly as they have been gained in many market segments if companies cannot back up their promises with adequate customer service. This book is a well-timed enquiry into the possibilities and limits of digital in the overall customer experience.*
>
> Mike Murphy, Front Row Speakers

Website – best practices

Almost every business across industry has a website. In a fast-changing medium such as on-line, *what good looks like* is a dynamic concept. The styles, look and feel for websites are constantly evolving. The best practices of today might well be out of date a year later. Nevertheless, there are a few key reminders as a checklist.

Because mobile plays such a big part in our world, most web developers now think 'mobile first'. They suggest designs and layout to suit a mobile phone upfront, rather than having it as an after-thought. 'Dynamic sites' adapt their shapes and formats to suit devices of all sizes.

In the early days of the Internet, almost all visitors to your site would enter through your home page initially. This is where you would illustrate in a general way who you are, what business you're in and an overview of your product suite. As search engines have become the more prominent entry-point to websites, every one of your pages needs to be welcoming and reassuring to visitors. A customer of your accountancy practice, for example, might search for tax advice and somehow land on a secondary page of your website. If you don't make it clear who and where you are and have some contact details, you may be in danger of losing that customer.

In the same way that customers in a department store are guided throughout the store with signage, a website should also consider how customers will navigate. Speed and ease of navigation are key success factors. Because of the dramatic growth in the use of mobile devices, businesses are now planning their websites with a 'mobile first' mindset. It used to be the reverse. Have your own logo on every page and a local contact number.

Before you go live with form-filling on your website, test it first. It might be a contact form or payment process, so ensure that it is easy and efficient. If customers make errors, do you highlight where they have made the error? Do you force customers to have to re-enter all their details again, or do the correct fields stay populated?

Here is a comprehensive checklist and best practice guide to website design:

Page layout

1. Pages should be designed in a way that is appealing and relevant to your target audience, i.e. corporate, entertaining, informative, etc.
2. Your header and logo should be consistent in all pages
3. Footer area should include contact details and copyright
4. Scrolling vertically is perfectly acceptable, but horizontal scrolling isn't
5. Not too much text or graphics; keep a balance with the amount of blank space
6. Responsive page layout is critical so that your site displays appropriately on desktop, tablet and mobile devices
7. Site should be compatible with all major search engines: Explorer, Edge, Google Chrome, Apple Safari, Firefox, Opera, etc.
8. All navigation hyperlinks are obvious and working
9. Most common fonts are Arial and Times New Roman
10. One font only rather than multiple fonts

Content

1. Problem statement is clear (in terms of the 'problem' that your product or service will address)
2. Landing/home page has compelling, meaningful and up to date information about your company and what you do
3. Content is organised in a consistent manner and easy to find

4. No typing or spelling errors
5. 'Call to action' is clear
6. Hyperlinks use a consistent set of colours

Colour and graphics

1. Colours are limited to four additional different colours if your main background colour is white
2. Colours are limited to three additional colours if your main background is a colour other than white
3. Your text colour should contrast appropriately with the background that it is in
4. Colour and graphics should be optimised to not slow down the navigation

Multimedia

1. Each video or audio clip should be appropriate and designed to enhance the message
2. Provide captions with each file and download time

Functionality

1. All internal hyperlinks work
2. All external hyperlinks work
3. All forms function as expected

It has been a privilege to have been associated with a brand such as Gieves & Hawkes and to have learned the subtle craft of exceeding a gentleman's expectations at every touchpoint of the customer journey from the master, Mr. Robert Gieve.

Technology has its place in providing excellent service, for that there is no doubt. It might be an emergency request for a black tie outfit to be delivered to an existing customer who has lost his luggage – and needs it for dinner at St Andrews that evening. Or simply an online shopper looking for a replacement for his favourite white shirt with no G&H store nearby. Regardless, the cloud is a marvellous way to reach our new and existing customers.

However, by far our most impressive online service tool is still the 'Book an Appointment' button. There is simply no substitute for an appointment with your tailor who guides you through one of life's truly unforgettable experiences, the art of making a bespoke suit that is just for you and never repeated. 'Clicks to Bricks' will certainly help ensure our customer service in-store continues for many years to come. Technology isn't service I believe that when used correctly, it can enhance any business, however traditional it may be.

Ray Clacher, CEO Gieves and Hawkes, Savile Row

SUMMARY

There is no doubting the role that technology has played in all our lives in recent times. It has enabled disruption for many industries and opportunity for others. The important point is to stay abreast of the trends that are relevant to your industry and particularly your customers. Keep an eye on what your competitors are doing and how your customers are changing. It's really difficult to stay ahead of the innovation curve, and most businesses therefore are reactive. Be careful; you can't have it all, so carefully edit and pick what is right for you.

This chapter highlights a checklist to ensure your customers' experience on-line is relevant to your brand.

Key Takeaways:

- Omni-channel (where customers can interact on various devices and platforms in the one single transaction) has taken over from multiple channels
- Retailers in particular have had more disruption than most – study that sector and see what you can learn that can be applied to your industry
- Customers are changing and embracing technology at a much faster rate than traditional businesses can provide for
- Personalisation is the way of the future, as technology enables businesses to tailor their marketing for different customer segments based on their behaviours and preferences

Key Questions For You:

- Do you have a strategy that embraces technology?
- Is your social media approach organised and consistent?
- Is your website up to date and responsive?

Watch For These Pitfalls:

- Don't react to new technology without checking for relevance to your industry and brand
- If your various initiatives are not joined up and cohesive, your customers may get mixed messages
- When you try something new, stick with it for an appropriate length of time

DELIVER PREMIUM ON THE TELEPHONE

Even in this age of digital communications, the telephone still plays a pivotal role in business. Whether it's to place an order with a supplier, check the status of an application, enquire about opening hours or book a table, the list goes on. The benefit of having an effective and professional telephone calls charter will endear you to your time-pressed customers and enhance your brand. When calling you on the telephone, your customer expects you to be an advisor, a problem-solver, a provider of information, a rescuer and a supporter. If the telephone is used as a customer experience tool, being mindful of these customer expectations will help your brand to stand out.

In this chapter, we explore best practices for incoming calls to your business and *what good looks like* for outgoing calls that your people make. You want to protect your organisation's good name. You'd like to enhance your quality of service and maybe even to sell. We'll also discuss how to deal with difficult calls, standards for transferring calls and standards for voicemail. Let's first discuss incoming calls.

Inbound calls

Customers will judge you initially on the waiting time for you to answer. If it's more than three rings, they'll feel impatient. Many organisations that have high volumes of inbound calls use an IVR system (interactive voice response). This is where callers are given a number of pre-recorded options and are invited to press a number to correspond to their preference. Examples include: press 1 if you are a current card holder, press 2 if you are enquiring about the status of your application, press 3 to report a lost card, and so on.

When this process was first introduced to the world there was a lot of resistance to it, especially with older folk. But this method is now growing in acceptance and has pretty much become the norm. It's interesting to see, however, that many premium brands don't use it. They believe that a 'real person' should be the first point of contact to give a more personal greeting. What's best for you?

The characteristics of a professional telephone operator include:

- Well prepared
- Caring, respectful, understanding
- Professional
- Knowledgeable
- Skilled at establishing needs
- Good listener
- Friendly
- Patient
- Calm
- Efficient
- Interested
- Clear

A trend has developed in many of the large multi-national organisations where operators refuse to give you their names. What's that all about? You find it a lot with telecoms organisations, who do much of their business on the telephone! Customers are invited to phone in with all sorts of queries. Yet when a problem develops and an escalation to a supervisor is requested, retrenchment is the default option and operators will refuse to give their names, quoting company policy. When it comes to making a complaint – well, that too becomes a pain in the neck and many complainers just don't bother.

The steps in handling incoming calls are:

1. Greeting
2. Establish reason for call
3. Agree on action
4. Transfer a call if necessary
5. Farewell greeting
6. Follow-up

1. *Greeting*

In the chapter on *people*, we talked about the importance of the initial effect of meeting somebody face to face and the importance of appearance. On the telephone, customers obviously can't see you, but they still get an impression which can be influenced and controlled by you if you get your tone right. Your tone should be friendly, upbeat, confident, clear and certainly not monotone. Your greeting should be short, crisp and to the point.

Some businesses try too hard to tick all the 'customer service' boxes. Here's an example of a greeting that has the best of intentions but is just too long: '*Hello, thank you for calling The Manor House Hotel and Country Club. This is Catherine speaking. How can I help you today?*' There are positives here, but in this time pressed world there is a danger of annoying the caller. One of the positives is that the employee gives her name.

2. *Establish reason for call*

Listen carefully to customers' opening requests. Admittedly, they might ramble on and take some time to get to the point, but you can control the call by asking specific questions to establish their needs. When you feel that you know what they want, repeat it back to them in summary form, to check your understanding.

If the request is brief and you can deal with it there and then, do so. Take responsibility yourself and give a clear suggestion or solution. Seek the caller's agreement that they are satisfied with your response. If there is a follow up action required, confirm what you will do and by when.

Perhaps let customers know that you are taking notes so that they know you are taking their call seriously.

3. *Agree on action*

If the request is more complex and you need time to get an answer, perhaps you might offer to call the customer back later. That gives you time to get the answer while not under pressure and also saves the customer waiting time. Make sure you get their name and telephone number and arrange a return call time.

If a customer wishes to speak to a colleague that is not available at this time, take a message and reassure the caller that you will pass the details immediately, taking name, organisation details and telephone number.

4. *Transfer the call*

Be careful when it comes to handing over the caller to another colleague. There are two things that often go wrong here. One is that the operator clicks the caller without informing the caller that they are being transferred. Callers are left waiting in anticipation to see if they have been cut off or transferred. The second and very frustrating issue is for the caller to have to repeat their whole story again to a new operator. As with a relay race, each operator should hand over the call to the next operator with care. That is much more reassuring for the caller. Here are the key watch-outs:

- Get the customer's name and purpose of the call
- Transfer, and make sure the caller does not have to repeat their whole story to the next operator
- If unsuccessful in getting your colleague, take customer's number and arrange a return call time

In the 1970s a clever idea in the form of pre-recorded electronic music was developed to ease callers' patience when asked to 'hold the line'. When operators asked you to hold while they fulfilled your request, you were treated to a few bars of 'Greensleeves' that sounded like it was recorded on a child's play instrument. It was novel at the time and it was designed to soothe the caller! Today, you'll often hear an advertisement for the company you are calling. Just be careful here as it says a lot about your brand.

5. Farewell greeting

At the end of the call, make sure that the customer doesn't feel rushed or dismissed. Use the caller's name, confirm agreed action (specific, achievable, time), thank the caller, and offer future help. Always let the customer hang up first!

6. Follow-up

Hanging up is not always the end of the call. If you have made a promise to the caller, you've got to follow up on any agreed actions. Make sure to form a habit around creating a diary note to follow up and complete the action. Return the call at the agreed time if you said you would.

> *The phone is an instrument of intrusion into order. It is a threat to control. Just when you think you are alone and safe, the call could come that changes your life. Or someone else's. It makes the same flat noise for everyone and gives no clues what's waiting there on the other end of the line. You can never be too careful.*
>
> Janice Galloway, Author

Outbound calls

In preparation for making outgoing calls, consider the customer's name and number, *who* should make the call, *what* information and resources are needed in advance, *where* the customer can be contacted, *when* suits the customer, *when* suits you, the caller, and *why* the call is being made. Is it to sell something or to give or seek information? Be conscious of the effect of this call on customer service.

The steps in handling outgoing calls are:

1. Greeting
2. Giving information
3. Leaving messages
4. Farewell greeting
5. Follow-up

1. Greeting

Don't assume that customers are available or willing to take your call when you call them. After introducing yourself, check their availability to chat. Say 'good morning' or 'good afternoon' and give your organisation, department and your own name. Ask for your customer by name and check their availability to talk. Then refer to the reason for the call or refer back to the initial query that prompted this call.

2. Giving information

If this is the first call to the customer, get to the point quickly. If the call is a follow up to a previous encounter, proceed with the call by updating on progress since the last call. As you give your information, check that the customer understands what you are saying. Also check that they are happy with your solution.

3. Leaving messages

If the caller is not available to take your call, listen carefully to any voice message on machine. Leave time, date, your company name, your department and your own name. If you are calling what you are certain to be a mobile phone, leave a discreet message. If you are calling a land-line that may be listened to by others, be very careful. Explain who you are, but do not leave a detailed message unless you are sure it is safe and appropriate to do so.

4. Farewell greeting

This is exactly the same as with inbound calls. At the end of the call you want to make sure that the customer doesn't feel rushed or dismissed. Use the customer's name, confirm agreed action (specific, achievable, time), thank the customer and offer future help. Always let the customer hang up first!

5. Follow-up

As with incoming calls, this is not always the end of the call. If you have made a promise to the caller, you've got to follow up on any agreed actions. Make sure to form a habit around creating a diary note to follow up and complete the action. Return the call at the agreed time if you said you would.

> *In the past, customers went to stores and location was everything. Retailing today is all about stores being adaptable and going to customers. This challenge can only be met by providing memorable and fruitful hospitality at all touchpoints – hence premium experience in all channels.*
>
> Werner Studer, Executive Director IGDS

SUMMARY

The telephone is a key moment of truth for your customers and they judge you and your brand every time they interact with you. It's time to prioritise this important medium and ensure that your customers get as positive an experience on the telephone as they would when they meet you in person.

SUMMARY

This chapter highlighted a protocol for both in-coming calls and outgoing calls.

Key Takeaways:

- Inbound calls should follow these steps:
  1. Greeting
  2. Establish reason for call
  3. Agree on action
  4. Transferring a call if necessary
  5. Farewell greeting
  6. Follow-up
- Outbound calls should follow these steps:
  1. Greeting
  2. Giving information
  3. Leaving messages
  4. Farewell greeting
  5. Follow-up

Key Questions For You:

- Should you use IVR or always have a real person answering your calls?
- Are your people trained or at least briefed on your telephone etiquette?

Watch For These Pitfalls:

- Dual conversations, where your operator causes confusion for your customer by talking to a colleague while within earshot of the customer
- Poor transfers between colleagues and/or customer being left to hold for too long
- Customer being given incorrect information or being fobbed off
- Poor manner, tone and follow up to promises by the operator
- Out of date voice mail message

Chapter Eight

Go the Extra Mile

'Going the extra mile' is a concept often used by organisations that pretty much does what it says: doing something over and above the customers' expectations. It might be a hotel offering to print off your airline boarding card as you check out of the hotel, a holiday company calling you after your holiday to see how you got on, etc.

Extra mile initiatives are only *extra mile* when they are not the norm for your industry or your positioning within that industry. For example, if you are a three star hotel, offering to print a boarding card is more typical of a five star hotel. What tends to happen is that one company in a sector might innovate with a new idea, and it is then copied by their competitors when the idea seems attractive and to be catching on. When that becomes the new base standard, it's no longer an *extra mile* service.

In this fast-changing world, the things that were initially seen as 'delighters' in an industry, eventually become mere 'satisfiers'. In other words, when one company innovates and comes up with an initiative that differentiates them, often that idea is then copied by the competition. Customers are then 'educated' to expect that as a norm. Hence, the customer experience overall has increased.

Here's an example: Superquinn in Ireland used to be an internationally recognised leader in customer service in their industry – grocery retailing. They were always innovating with new ideas and concepts to wow their customers. They were the first Irish retailer to have young messengers accompany their customers to their cars with umbrellas when it rained. They had exclusivity with the concept for a few months, until every competitor eventually bought umbrellas too. So even though Superquinn were the first to do it, in a short space of time it became the new norm and was no longer seen to be *going the extra mile*. Now imagine that tiny example multiplied across all industries.

Be careful how you present your services. Know the standard in your sector.

Many organisations misuse and misplace the expression 'going the extra mile'. There is nothing wrong with the phrase and the sentiment per se. It's just that if you focus your energy on extra mile initiatives without taking care of the basics in the first place, it simply won't work and have the effect you wish for. In fact, it could even go against you. The word 'extra' gives a strong hint that it's got to be over and above! Over and above what in particular? That has to be the basics in the first place! Here's an example that explains that little piece of mumbo-jumbo.

Let's go back again to Superquinn to illustrate the point. Founded and led by its owner, Feargal Quinn, they developed a reputation for great service that greatly exceeded that of its competitors. At their peak, their mantra was '*Come for the prices and stay for the service*'. They were not the cheapest by any stretch of the imagination. Their prices were probably slightly higher at the time, but that price difference was compensated for with premium service. Their reputation was so good that retailers from all over the world came on field visits to learn from them.

Feargal himself was a master and role model for great service. He frequently got publicity for being the voice of the consumer and made a big deal of being seen on the shop floor talking to customers. As a result of talking and listening to their customers, Superquinn invented lots of *firsts* in grocery retailing, such as removing sweets from the checkouts, giving double points on your loyalty card if you found a price error, and as mentioned earlier, walking you to your car with an umbrella when it rained. (Keep this umbrella in mind for a few minutes!)

However, despite this fantastic focus on the customer, they weren't immune to operational things going wrong. They also suffered occasionally from inefficient staff, housekeeping standards not being up to scratch and key lines being out-of-stock.

So what? A customer went to Superquinn for his weekly grocery supplies one week with a request from his family to also get Kilmeaden Cheddar (the No1 Irish cheese), but it was unfortunately out of stock. He went home and faced the wrath of his family, and vowed to not let that happen again. Through habit and convenience, he returned to the same store the following very wet Saturday to do his weekly shop – with the same request for cheese from his family. Guess what? Kilmeaden Cheddar was out of stock again. The customer sulked for the rest of the visit but continued shopping and eventually made it to the checkout. The bag packer at the checkout kindly offered to accompany him to his car with an umbrella as it was a wet day. Can you just imagine what he was tempted to say to the bag packer with the umbrella?

> *Businesses that go that extra mile, provide an outstanding customer service and give a unique experience to their customers – will succeed.*
>
> Feargal Quinn speaking at the GS1 Forum

The point here is that if you don't get the basics right, the extra mile initiatives are seen as a cynical and insincere gesture. Yes, they are great if and when the basics are in place – first time, on time and every time. See the basics as the foundation and extra mile things as further building blocks. When you ask typical customers what their expectations are, they seldom declare *extra mile* things as their primary need. But for sure, if you ask customers about their poor *customer experiences*, they will almost always quote the silly basic things, such as rudeness, no call-back as promised, etc. Most Kara research studies will support this.

In fact, research studies of complaints show that most faults and issues are to do with these basic elements and expectations, not the extra mile initiatives. There is a strong possibility that your competitors are also getting it wrong on the basics. Maybe that's where you can excel with superior customer experience, by simply delivering the basics day in and day out. When you are confident that as an organisation you are delivering the basics on time every time, then perhaps the extra mile initiatives can be added on top.

This story serves as a significant signpost for your business in helping you define what *great customer experience* is. Returning to the differentiation debate from earlier, if you put most of your focus and energy into ensuring the basics are right every time, that in itself will make you different from your competitors. That is where your competitors are also getting it wrong. When you know that your basics are consistently in place without risk, then and only then should you work on extra mile ideas.

Business books on customer service, such as *Hug Your Customers* by Jack Mitchell, are loaded with great stories of where companies went above and beyond – i.e. went the extra mile. That is indeed admirable and inspiring and makes for great reading. Such stories are great for getting good PR and for storytelling. But to re-iterate, the basics come first.

Here is a sample list of extra-mile services that might work for a hotel or retail:

Tourists:

- Menus translated to languages to suit your tourist customers
- Language services
- Internal ads in key languages
- Website in key languages
- Luggage rental
- Shipping and packing
- Tourist gurus
- Deliver to hotel
- Concierge desk
- Airline check-in from hotel or store
- Support for non-shoppers in family – three generations
  - Wheelchairs
  - Crèche
- Hotel room to suit the whole family

All others:

- ATM, Bureau de Change
- Key-cutting, dry-cleaning, flower delivery
- Deliveries
- Tailoring
- Printing – stationery and photos
- Interior decorating
- Beauty advice – unbiased – non-brand
- Home makeover
- Installation of tech purchases in home
- Collections experts – taste creators
- Customisation
- Education/classes
- Fashion/styling
- Cookery classes
- Barista and sommelier classes

- Christmas home styling and dressing
- Private shopping
- VIP card
- Gift guru
- Wedding planning
- Corporate gifting
- Follow up telephone call after significant purchase
- Career guidance
- Catering – in-store and external
- Introduction to luxury shopping – to raise comfort
  - Web seminar
  - On-site
  - 'What is Personal Shopping' and expectations

SUMMARY

'Going the extra mile' is a nice idea, as it suggests that you do something that the customer didn't expect. But if the fundamental basics are not in place to start with, extras might be seen as a cynical exercise on your part. If you focus on getting the basics right day in, day out, then perhaps that in itself might be your differentiator.

Undoubtedly your competitors get the basics wrong on a regular basis and you might just blow them out of the water if you avoid that trap. When you get to a point of delivering consistently great service and you know that you are delivering the basics every day, then consider what additional 'extra mile' things might wow your customer.

Key Takeaways:

- Get the basics right day in, day out before you think about 'extra mile' ideas
- Extra mile activities are great provided you can deliver on them consistently
- When the basics are embedded as the norm in your culture, find additional new things to wow your customers

Key Questions For You:

- How consistent are you in delivering the basics every day?
- What does 'going the extra mile' look like at your various touchpoints?

Watch For These Pitfalls:

- Don't over-promise if you can't be sure to deliver as promised, consistently
- Don't let extra mile initiatives dominate internal conversations as they may cause the eye to move off the ball

Part Three

How to Deliver Great Customer Experience, Consistently

Chapter Nine

Customer-ise Your Culture

We know from previous chapters what great companies with a reputation for great customer experience do. But how do they achieve consistency and do it every day? If the concept and commercial value of great customer experience is as obvious and clear as is made out in this book, why do customers get consistently great experiences with one company and regularly poor experience with another?

For clarity, there is a difference between *poor service* (promises unfulfilled) and *less service* (as you would see between a full-service airline and a low-cost, low fares, no-frills airline). Just because the low-cost airline doesn't give free drinks doesn't mean that the service is bad. Because of the company's brand DNA and how they position themselves, customers know to expect a different proposition. *Poor service* is where a customer has a reasonable expectation of a particular standard and that falls short.

In previous chapters, we looked at *what* customer experience is. We saw that the brand DNA sets the context for everything about your customer experience proposition. We saw that processes, rules and resources are usually determined at central management level. We talked about the 3-legged stool as a framework for working out *what good looks like* and how that affects the customers' experience – *product, people and place*. How do we ensure that all our teams are giving great service consistently, even when they're not being observed?

It's time that we talked about *how* this is delivered. What does it take for an organisation to ensure that the agreed standards are delivered relentlessly, every single day? It's all about *corporate culture*. Culture is the key ingredient and the thread that ensures the best link between the experiences *we want* customers to get and what they *actually* get.

Culture

When we think of culture, we often think of the cultures we experience in different countries around the world. There are countless examples of where culture is deeply rooted in national identities. We experience it through language, food, style of dress, religion, beliefs, fears, architecture, media, customs, lifestyle, family, music and sport.

If you were blindfolded and then dropped into any well-known country in the world, you'd know very quickly where you were, and not just because of the language that's spoken there. France is known around the world for its love of fine food and the dining experience. Working-class Filipinos that move abroad to earn money have their children reared by their parents. Irish people are known for their warmth and hospitality. Emiratis are known for their tolerance in an age of 'east meets west'.

Gestures can also mean different things in different cultures. In Western countries a handshake should be firm and last for a few seconds. That same approach might be considered aggressive in the Middle East. Similarly, in Japan the preference is for people to bow and put their own hands together in a praying position when greeting. The 'thumbs up' gesture means 'okay' in some cultures, while in others it can be interpreted as a rude gesture. Eye contact is considered friendly and welcoming by some and intrusive by others. Smiling is universally seen to be friendly, and yet some cultures are more aloof at first.

Within nationalities, culture can vary further across politics, communities, associations, education bodies and even families. At a macro level there will be consistencies, such as language and maybe even religion. But there might be nuanced differences across all other facets.

Because culture tends to drive consistency of style and behaviours, we can also recognise the culture of some global organisations very quickly. Apple are famous for their innovation. Virgin are consistently people focused and friendly. Disney are totally customer-centric in all that they do. However, that culture message also applies to some negative aspects, such as with Enron for their personal and corporate greed, or Volkswagen for the emissions scandal. Let's not forget about the bad practices of some banks with PPI mis-selling, the LIBOR scandal and money-laundering.

> *In a world that's changing faster than ever before, one thing that has not and will never change is the need to provide the best experience possible for your customers. It's the only way to ensure your customers spend today, come back again and recommend you to their friends.*
>
> *Consistency has always been the biggest challenge and ensuring that your employees are engaged is a critical enabler of that.*
>
> Ross O'Neill, Managing Director RGON Insights

What is corporate culture?

We need to position culture in the overall business mix. Here is how it fits.

Imagine a scenario where you win the lotto and you invest money in a business. The ultimate metric of success is a collection of key performance indicators (KPIs) such as sales, profit, return on capital, market share, customer satisfaction and employee satisfaction. Those metrics are directly affected by whether customers have a good experience or not. That experience is enabled by the internal system working in synchronicity: teamwork, communications, operations, etc.

Underpinning all this is a clear vision and mission that serves as a North Star keeping the business on track. That's the *why* or the 'raison d'etre' of the business. A clearly defined strategy determines *what* the key pillars of success will be in the coming years ahead. An appropriate and well-considered structure describes *who* will do what and when. But even with a clearly defined strategy, there is no guarantee that the plan will be executed effectively or in keeping with the intent of stakeholders. So what's missing?

In any organisation that has more than one person, you will get inconsistencies in management style, attitudes, behaviours, decision-making and so on. What if one of those people has a natural affinity to being nice to customers, but the second person is less so? Straight away, customers will get inconsistent messages. Now multiply that by the number of people or departments in your own organisation and you'll get a sense of the risk of not defining your culture. What if each person on your team had a different perspective of how to treat each other on the team? What if the leaders were allowed to just be themselves with no guidance?

What's missing in this list, however, is *how* things should get done. That's culture. Every organisation has a culture, regardless of whether it was proactively defined or not. In fact in most cases, the culture just evolves. But if that culture is not thought and planned for, an organisation will develop one anyway. In the absence of a structured approach to developing one, there is a risk of ambiguity, mixed messages and confusion, inefficiencies, poor customer service and disappointing financial results.

One way or another, culture drives consistency of either good or poor customer experiences. The challenge and opportunity therefore is to consider what the right culture is for you. It should take due consideration of the ambitions of the shareholders, heritage, the brand DNA, the broader marketplace, customer expectations, competitor activity and the strategy.

Organisations that have been around for a while tend to have a strong identifiable culture, even if it is not intended or defined. Because culture is also affected by what is going in the world at large at a given time, organisations should be prepared to review their culture from time to time, to accommodate relevant and appropriate changes. That is not to suggest that culture should change often, like strategy or business goals. It doesn't and shouldn't. But from time to time, trends do emerge that prompt a review.

The banking scandals and the global financial crises certainly prompted the need for a change of culture in banking. The dynamics in a sector can change as well.

Take retail for example. Retail as a sector has probably experienced more change than most other sectors. There has been so much technological advancement in retail, and with the swing from bricks and mortar stores to on-line shopping, the thinking in traditional retailers must change. That's culture.

People change over time. There is much talk and focus on Millennials and how they are different. If you agree that Millennials want to attach themselves to companies with a strong social conscience, you may need to think about that if you wish to attract them as employees. The tech companies like Google and Facebook have also created an expectation of a certain kind of 'cool' workplace and work-life balance. Your employer brand needs to reflect a culture that is right for you as an organisation and that will attract the right talent.

A well thought out culture sets the tone for:

- Human resource management: people get hired, fired, rewarded and recognised and communicated with according to what is valued and regarded as appropriate.
- Marketing: all messaging in terms of style, content and tone is influenced by culture.
- Operations: things get executed effectively and efficiently or not, depending on the organisation culture
- Decisions and processes: these are influenced by culture. For example, if your customer is at the heart of your culture, then processes around how complaints are handled will be effortless for the customer.

Today's customer has access to a multitude of information which enables them to make choices about what they buy and where they buy. Most products are now commoditized and it is rare that customers are compelled to buy from one particular source simply because the product does not exist elsewhere. So how do you make sure customers choose you over your competitors?

Think of the product and the process of getting these to customers as a hygiene factor; get it wrong and you've likely lost a customer. Get it right and no one really thanks you. Operational excellence and product standards form the minimum expectation.

The key to creating loyalty to your brand is delivering end to end customer experiences that exceed expectations. But how do you know what each customer expects? Engage with customers, listen to them and use information wisely to create the experience. But that on its own, is unlikely to differentiate you from your real competitors.

In my experience, organisations who use creativity and instinct, while constantly driving to do things better and better, deliver the most unique experiences that amaze customers. They push boundaries to create the element of surprise and they constantly develop that experience to stay ahead. From my time as HRD in

> *Selfridges, I know first-hand that a culture of operational excellence and creativity is undoubtedly what makes it the best department store in the world!*
>
> Maria Stanford, Director Stanford James

Culture could almost be described as the software of the mind and is often defined like this:

1. Vision and mission (we've touched on this already – brand DNA)
2. Artefacts (practical and physical embodiment of the brand and culture)
3. Beliefs, stories, jokes and language
4. *'The way we do things around here'* (and this is the *how*)

Let's look at each in turn.

1. Vision and mission – what do you want to be when you grow up?

Do you remember being asked as a child what you want to be when you grow up? Most kids have dreams and ambitions to be something or other, and indeed that may change many times as they grow through the years. Having that ambition is very helpful as it gives them guidance and direction. Some kids follow their dreams right through school and university and become a version of what they aspired to and longed for. Some other kids are not quite as committed and may well end up successful regardless – but perhaps not as they had dreamt for.

In the simplest terms, a clearly defined *vision* and *mission* give direction in an organisation for all who follow. Picture yourself setting out on a journey where you have all sorts of choices, such as turning left, turning right, or going straight. If you have a plan, the decision for what turn to take is easy. While that is blatantly obvious, it's surprising how many organisations don't have that clarity.

We touched on this in Chapter 2. Remember, for example, statements like:

Amazon	To be earth's most customer centric company; to build a place where people can come to find and discover anything they might want to buy online
Apple	Apple is committed to bringing the best personal computing experience to students, educators, creative professionals and consumers around the world through its innovative hardware, software and Internet offerings

You can be sure that those statements took hours, if not days, to finalise and wordsmith. Some of the key words in Amazon's statement include *customer centric, anything they want* and *online*. These three elements alone make it very clear to all Amazon employees that when they do something, make a recommendation, or change a process, it should be done with full consideration for its effect on the customer.

Goals tend to be what you are trying to deliver in a shorter time frame, but a *vision* is a declaration of where you want your organisation to be in the long term. A vision statement is often described as what you want your organisation to be when it grows up. They tend to have an inward focus and reflect the ambition for the organisation. For example, Selfridges UK want *to be the destination for the most extraordinary customer experiences*. That is saying something about where they want to be positioned and measured against their competition. It's why they exist. Vision statements often start with the words '*We will be*'.

To make it less fluffy, a vision becomes even more tangible when it has metrics attached to it for varying time horizons. Those metrics will include all the obvious financials, such as market share, revenue, profit, return on investment, customer satisfaction ratios, and employee satisfaction ratios. But remember that metrics can change every year – the vision and mission don't. Another point is that the vision should be aspirational and not just a statement of where you are right now. It should challenge, inspire passion and motivate the teams to reach for something that you don't currently have.

A *Mission* (sometimes called *Purpose*) is a high-level statement declaring how the *vision* will be achieved and has more of an outward focus. In the *Mission Impossible* films, Tom Cruise and his colleagues are given missions to complete – *if they choose to accept them*! Once again looking at Selfridges UK, they believe they *are here to surprise, amaze and amuse our customers – and everyone is welcome.*

The combination of a *vision* and a *mission* are a very powerful overview of the ambition of any company. If you're struggling with trying to decide what the difference is between *vision* and *mission*, don't get too hung up on it. If you study the statements from some of the world's greatest companies, you'll even see inconsistencies in them. If you are satisfied that you have come up with a *North Star* for your business that sets a long term realistic challenge to inspire, motivate and give clarity – that's all you need. As mentioned, the metrics will make the aspiration tangible.

If your organisation does have a vision and mission, you're not off the hook yet. Ask yourself how well it is communicated. Having the statements articulated and written down is only the start. They then need to be used to help shape the strategy, the structure and the projects that are undertaken day to day. For a start, ensure that they are communicated to everyone in the business. All employees should know these statements by heart and be able to tell a stranger in an elevator or at a party what the business is all about. Perhaps you might develop internal collateral such as posters, mouse mats, paper weights, notebooks, pens, or whatever is appropriate to your brand DNA. They might also inform the individual *Objective Setting* process, where managers are given objectives to deliver in a certain time frame.

At the very least, when making decisions or changes in your business, develop a habit of checking the effect of that decision on your organisation's ambition. This will help you decide what to do and what *not* to do.

When the global economy goes through a significant change, such as a boom or a downturn, the ripple effect can cause lots more to change. The global crash of

2008 and beyond, for example, caused many closures worldwide. Among those that survived, there are few of them that have not changed at some significant level. What effect would that then have on *vision* and *mission*? In many cases, the businesses changed dramatically. Here's a way to look at that.

Imagine trying to assemble a jigsaw without access to the lid on the box to guide you. You might give it a try by starting with the corners and working your way in. But before long you will be very frustrated and will want to throw it out the window! How much quicker, easier and more motivating would it be if you had the *lid on the box* to guide you?

Now picture this. Before the global financial crash, your employees were given a number of pieces for a metaphorical jigsaw that were appropriate to the business at that time. Over the years, many of them probably became quite good at assembling their pieces of the overall jigsaw. With a strong sense of achievement, they may even have got a bonus or other forms of recognition over time.

Then when the global financial crash came and businesses had to re-evaluate and change, 'the lid on the box' may have changed too. Unless you communicated that change and made it very clear, your people were probably still coming to work with their original pieces of the old jigsaw and assembling them as they always did. And of course, they were probably getting it wrong in the context of the new jigsaw! Picture the consternation that would have caused as your people tried to work out why they were getting it wrong!

> *Organisations get the behaviours they deserve.*
>
> Anon

In the last century, IBM was the biggest computer 'manufacturer' in the world. In simple terms, their strategy was to buy in and assemble components for PCs made by other manufacturers, then to put the IBM badge on the finished products. That worked for some time and helped them to become No1 in the world. At the same time, other new brands like Dell adapted the same strategy but had a different and better supply chain model. Consequently, IBM almost became the biggest crash in corporate financial history. But they caught themselves just in time. They re-evaluated the competitive market and re-invented themselves as a computer services and solutions company. While still manufacturing, they are now the global No1 again – but in a new space.

The IBM Mission Statement says: *At IBM, we strive to lead in the invention, development and manufacture of the industry's most advanced information technologies, including computer systems, software, storage systems and microelectronics. We translate these advanced technologies into value for our customers through our professional solutions, services and consulting businesses worldwide.*

That re-invention was a significant milestone in the life of IBM. It was carefully planned with a massive organisation-wide *change management programme*. Their new vision and mission was an essential part of that change and they made sure that the whole organisation was familiar with the new '*lid on the box*'.

2. *Artefacts, visuals and symbols*

Artefacts are such things as the company logo, livery, corporate colours, employee dress code, marketing campaigns, brochures, websites, fixturing, packaging/bag, and transport – all determined by the brand DNA.

Some retailers, for example, do not use plastic bags and their delivery vans are electric. Both initiatives, by the way, also support their stances on environmental awareness and Corporate Social Responsibility.

Artefacts say a lot about an organisation's culture. You can tell from these artefacts if they are traditional or modern, friendly or aloof, young or old, hierarchical or democratic – the list goes on. You can also tell a lot from the standards in a company's reception area, store or general office environment. If you enter a sloppy work area, you can tell that the culture is less about pride or respect.

Google are famous for their bean bags and relaxed work environment, which send strong messages to their own employees. Now that is all very well, but their back-office areas are not customer-facing. The reason for saying that is that there is an employee engagement paradigm that refers to the *Google effect*. Google have such a reputation for how they treat employees that they are the envy of many others. However, given what is known publicly about Google and their culture, undoubtedly they'd replicate that approach if they had a B2C environment.

3. *Beliefs, jokes, stories and language*

In a recent Kara workshop with a group of motor dealers, customers were referred to as 'punters'. That is a term that usually refers to gamblers. What has that got to do with a customer buying a car?

Lots of companies have a collection of 'in-jokes' and stories that reflect the style of the company. Some of those stories might create a sense of pride or fear, if for example, the stories are about how people have been treated, hired or fired. Externally, the stories might illustrate a modern or innovative culture, such as those at Google, Facebook and other tech giants. Ryanair is the largest airline in Europe and opinion is divided about their culture. For years they seemed to be almost dismissive of customers and had a reputation for poor internal relations. Whether they are truths or myths, such stories gather momentum and perception can become the reality.

4. *'The way we do things around here'*

It's all very well having processes, rules and documents that articulate what great customer experience is. But unless the *behaviours* are lined up with this, the customer will see it as cynical and not believable. So what drives behaviour?

Rather than do a deep dive into the world of psychology, let's make this easy. Customers either *receive* or *don't receive* great customer experiences. The word *receive* implies an *action* of some sort. An action requires behaviour to carry it out. Then where does *behaviour* come from?

To take a simple and conversational look at behaviours, consider the following.

Values

We all live to a set of *values*. Here is a short list of typical values that some or most of us will claim that we live by:

Respectful	Honest	Liberal
Frugal	Ethical	Fair
Caring	Benevolent	Adaptable
Adventurous	Reliable	Strong work ethic

Your core values drive your behaviours. By way of example:

1. Take the value *respectful*. Imagine you are sitting while travelling on a very full bus. Imagine that at the next stop, a person less able than you gets on. Because you are *respectful*, you will most likely offer your seat to that person. This is an instinctive action on your part. There is no checklist to go through. You just do it.
2. *Liberal* suggests a tolerance of the views of others and their ways of doing things. If you are liberal, you are likely to listen and be less likely to force your opinion on another person.
3. If you have a *strong work ethic* as a value, you will want to work for your living rather than relying on state welfare.

In short, values drive behaviours. In all three examples here, you won't wait till you're told what to do. You just do it instinctively.

Undoubtedly, you and your organisation want a certain set of behaviours to be instinctive and to be evident all the time. If you want a set of relevant and appropriate behaviours that are guaranteed to ensure that your customers get consistent great experiences, even when you're not around, you should define what those behaviours are. Then find a set of linked values that are likely to invoke those behaviours.

In large organisations where employees might come from many different nationalities with differing backgrounds and cultures, there is a risk. Countries, religions and races often have distinct cultures that differentiate them. For example, in some cultures it is the norm to say 'please' and 'thank you' and in some cultures, it is not the norm. In some cultures it is acceptable to make eye contact with everyone, and in some cultures it is not. It is of course welcome that cultures cross over and that organisations select their people on merit rather than on where they hail from. But if you want your customers to be greeted with eye contact, that might be an issue for some of your team applicants. Therefore, that needs to be addressed up front at the recruitment stage.

Organisations should decide on a set of core values to determine the typical behaviours they want to see in their people. While not exclusively, values are the main driver of culture.

> *We believe that it's really important to come up with core values that you can commit to. And by commit, we mean that you're willing to hire and fire based on them. If you're willing to do that, then you're well on your way to building a company culture that is in line with the brand you want to build.*
>
> Tony Hsieh, CEO, Zappos

What does it take to ensure you get the behaviours that you deserve? After deciding on what great customer experience looks like using the 3 Ps, here are the steps to ensure the behaviours are consistent:

1. Define the values and articulate the types of behaviours that are relevant and linked to each one
2. Ensure your leaders are living the values by role-modelling those behaviours
3. Hire new people according to these values
4. Communicate and train your people to know, understand and live the values
5. Monitor your people against the agreed values and behaviours
6. Measure internally to what extent the company is living the values
7. Make your people accountable for their behaviours
8. Reward your people for living them – have consequences if they don't

1. Define the values and behaviours

Organisations that already have a set of values should be complimented for having them. But too often they are simply a collection of words on a wall sign or a website and are not used beyond that. If you don't have a set of values, take time to agree them by consensus across all stakeholders.

Then for each value, make a list of indicative behaviours to illustrate what is meant by that value. There is no way that you could possibly list every single relevant behaviour, but the indicative list will provide a framework.

2. Ensure your leaders are living the values by role-modelling those behaviours

It is often said that children learn much more from 'what is caught' than 'what they are taught'. In other words, they are more likely to adopt behaviours that they see regularly than behaviours based on what you may say to them. For example, imagine parents telling a child not to smoke – as they themselves smoke cigarettes.

In the same context, employees are like children. They are more likely to behave as their role models do. If they see their boss speaking unkindly to a subordinate, they will rationalise that it is okay for them to do that too. After all, the boss has been promoted with that as a style. That must mean that it is okay!

Or imagine if a boss is persistently good with customers, clearly prioritising customer service as an ingredient for success – what do you think the employees will believe?

> *Good customer service begins at the top. If your senior people don't get it, even the strongest links further down the line can become compromised.*
>
> Richard Branson

3. Hire new people according to these values

When recruiting for new people, take time in advance of the process to consider the key criteria for the role that you're recruiting for. When preparing for the interview, consider what you are looking for in terms of the main tasks of the job and the appropriate behaviours you expect to see. Use the applicant's CV to guide you through their career to date. But be careful. CVs tend to be a chronological sequence of career highlights that don't usually focus explicitly on values and behaviours. You'll need to formulate other questions to establish their value and their fit with yours.

4. Communicate and train your people to know, understand and live the values

To bring the values to life in your organisation, you might consider an ongoing communications and training programme as an appropriate vehicle. The initial induction training programme for new hires is the starting point. The values and the indicative behaviours should play a big part in this early training so that the message is clear from the start.

Other communications and training channels should always include a reference to the values. You might also consider some collateral on the walls, screen savers on desktops, mouse mats, or other such opportunities. Your internal newsletter is an added vehicle for re-enforcing the values.

5. Monitor your people against the agreed values and behaviours

Having set the values and related behaviours and communicated them to everyone, watch to see that they are being respected by all. Observe employees when in meetings or in one-to-one conversations. Listen to how they speak to customers and to each other.

6. Measure internally to what extent the company is living the values

An annual or bi-annual Employee Engagement Survey is essential for getting a real insight into what extent employees are living up to the values. When constructing the survey, add some relevant questions linked to the values. One of the best engagement survey providers out there is a company called RGON Insights, who have a unique *cause and effect* approach. They don't just focus on giving you a score; they are totally focused on helping you to improve engagement. And that requires action plans.

7. Make your people accountable for their behaviours

Include values in your formal performance reviews. Discussions with your employees about performance results (numbers) are of course essential, but you might also have discussions with the employees about 'how' they achieved the results in terms of behaviours. For example, if one of your values refers to respect, but one high-results employee has been treating colleagues atrociously, that is not acceptable and needs to be dealt with.

8. Reward your people for living your values – have consequences if they don't

When you observe your people living the values with related behaviours, let them know that you have observed them. If you acknowledge it with them and show your appreciation, they will be motivated to continue doing that.

Likewise, people need to know that there are consequences for inappropriate behaviours. When you spot inappropriate behaviours, you should let people know as soon as possible that they are not living the values.

Leadership

It would be remiss to close off on culture without talking about leadership. If you follow all the thinking and steps above, you will start to develop a culture that is right for your organisation, but that is only the start of it. To ensure the culture is lived through the required behaviours, leaders need to be on board. Just in the same way that parents cannot successfully scold a child for a behaviour that they themselves do (such as smoking), leaders must model the right behaviours.

Leaders have a dramatic effect on culture and the behaviours of their people. Look at Richard Branson (Virgin) and Michael O'Leary (Ryanair). Both have very different styles and are the faces of their respective brands. On the face of it, which one puts the customer first? Which one portrays respect for their own employees?

Kara core values

In all the culture change projects undertaken by Kara over the years, there are three trends worth pointing out. These are a result of surveys, focus groups and one-to-one conversations across industry, in organisations of all sizes.

- *Engaging*: When your employees are engaged they will be more highly productive. They will have great pride in the company. They will give better service and they will work harder. They also show themselves to stay longer and indeed to recommend you as an employer to their friends.
- *Accountable*: There are many examples of organisations where there is too much ambiguity around roles and responsibilities. So much falls between stools, and

when people are not encouraged to deliver projects against appropriate metrics, apathy and blame can set in.
- *Customer centric*: If an organisation is more focused internally on their own affairs, systems and processes than on the customers' changing needs, that is a recipe for disaster.

In addition to good strategy, when these characteristics are present in a culture, projects get executed with more efficiency and financial results are more likely to be achieved. Whatever culture you decide to shape for your organisation, watch for these three pillars as a minimum.

Cross-departmental surveys

In order to give consistently great customer service, all the departments in an organisation need to treat each other as customers too. This is known as *internal service*. Using the values, consider crafting a cross-departmental survey of those values. Here is how that works.

For each value, identify, say, three or four key behaviours that indicate how that value should be lived. For example, if *accountability* is one of your values, you might identify the following behaviours: *'takes ownership for actions'*, *'delivers on time'*, and *'involves the appropriate people'*.

If you have five values and three questions per value, that gives you a survey with fifteen questions. Then distribute the survey to each department, asking them as a team in that department to rate other departments against these fifteen questions. All the results will then be collated anonymously, to give an overall score for each department.

When the feedback is distributed, departments will then see how they are viewed by other parts of the business, giving them a focus for corrective action and improvements.

SUMMARY

To achieve consistency with great customer experience, organisations need to have a culture that supports it. Training on its own is simply not enough. If the culture does not support a strong customer centric ethos, then customer experience will not be prioritised. Lip-service may be paid to it, but when the pressure is on, it will be forgotten.

Culture should be designed to support your vision, mission and long-term strategy. If you don't proactively design and articulate your desired culture, one will form anyway... one that you may or may not be happy with.

Every organisation has a culture, regardless of whether it was designed or not. But a culture that is proactively designed and delivered by you, will help significantly to support your organisation ambition.

SUMMARY

More and more organisations recognise that a clearly defined set of *values* are the key driver of a desired culture, provided they are lived day to day.

Key Takeaways:

- Culture is like software of the mind
- Culture is made up of vision, mission, artefacts, stories, behaviours and processes. Take time to define your culture to support your ambition and long-term strategy.
- Behaviours come from values. For each value, define a set of indicative behaviours so that your team know what is expected of them.
- An effective Kara Culture has three pillars: *engaging, accountable*, and *customer centric.*

Key Questions For You:

- Do you have clearly defined vision and mission statements that reflect your ambition in a new and dynamically changing world?
- If you have a set of values already, are they truly being lived daily? Are they still relevant today?
- If you don't have a set of values, how will you determine what they should be?

Watch For These Pitfalls:

- Progressive leaders will usually support the concept of values, but will often fail to model them themselves
- Many established organisations do have a set of values but regularly miss the effect they can have on achieving the strategy

Chapter Ten

Build a Service Recovery and Complaints Management Programme

Carlsberg, now the fourth largest beer manufacturer in the world, is a Danish institution. As a quality brand, they are also known for their intelligent and humorous TV advertisements. One ad many years ago depicted an employee walking along an often unused corridor in Carlsberg Head Office. Hearing an old style telephone ringing relentlessly in the distance, he tried to figure out where it was coming from. He established the sound coming from behind a very old door with a fading sign that read: *Complaints Dept.* The guy went in, found the old telephone on a desk, and scraping back the dust, he answered it. It turned out that the caller had dialled the wrong number.

The inference is of course that Carlsberg never receive complaints.

For the rest of us, the concept of never having a complaint is as unlikely as it is unreal. Even with the best will in the world and with the best products and services from the best iconic companies, everyone gets a complaint at some time or other. It might not even be an issue that was caused by your company. Perhaps you were relying on a third party delivery company or supplier... or there was an accident on the motorway... or a storm caused a power failure.

Let us accept and acknowledge that things will go wrong and you will get complaints. Your challenge is two-fold – to prevent them as much as possible, but also to address them favourably when they happen.

When it comes to handling and managing complaints, there is no room for complacency. In an earlier chapter, we saw that customers will defect when they have an issue unresolved, which in turn has serious implications for customer retention and your future sales potential. An effective *complaints management process* is an essential focus for any organisation of any size.

How often have you experienced a service provider handling complaints badly? It seems to be more the norm that they do it badly rather than effectively. Think about it. The customer may deliver the complaint awkwardly or even badly and that can cause defensiveness in the service provider or tempers to flare. That is indeed unfortunate, but why should we expect the customers to get it right? Why should we expect that they have the natural skill to deliver their feedback in a professional way? They have had a bad experience and their emotions are high. With that, their expectations go up and up.

As a service provider, you may have failed to get it right and please the customer the first time. However, if your organisation approached this from the right mindset, you'd see that the customer is actually giving you a second opportunity to get it right the first time!

You'll have seen or experienced bad complaint handling in your own world even as a consumer. It might be a retail salesperson tutting when they see a customer walk towards them with a bag, or a waiter who refuses to accept that the steak was not as ordered. No matter what, to act in any way other than welcoming and positively is simply daft.

There used to a well known piece of generic feedback that suggested that when customers are happy with their experience, they tell an average of five people. The converse was that when they are unhappy, they tell nine people, due to their emotions being more alert. But that was before social media! In a show of hands in a recent Kara Academy Workshop, 80% of participants admitted to using TripAdvisor before planning a trip. So that old 5:9 is way out of date now. Who knows what the numbers are? But for sure, they've got to be scary.

When an organisation looks on negative feedback in a positive way with good process and culture, the results are usually good. There is further evidence to show that customers who had a bad experience that was handled well actually became stronger advocates and ambassadors for the brand.

There is also the cost issue. Data will show that when complaints are handled badly they end up costing the service provider hard cash. However, when the service provider is honest and professional early on, the double win in terms of a relieved customer and no financial cost is obvious.

EPCAF – a model for service recovery

Customers seldom have the effective communication skills to make a complaint, or indeed, don't always know who to make the complaint to. For that reason, it makes sense that everyone in your organisation should know how to recognise a complaint in the first place and should also have the skills to handle it effectively. EPCAF is an effective model that will work in almost every situation and that can be learned by all who interface with a customer.

E – Empathise

Customers are very often irate that they have had an issue in the first place. Maybe they gave a gift to a friend that turned out to be faulty and are now embarrassed. Maybe they ordered the new table for a very important dinner party or perhaps they missed their flight because of you. In a B2B world, imagine if your customer was waiting on your raw materials to fulfil an important customer order.

We as service providers should stop and think about the effect of our failures on our customers.

> *When you show deep empathy towards others, their defensive energy goes down, and positive energy replaces it. That's when you can get more positive in solving problems.*
>
> Stephen Covey

In fairness, not all complaints are as a result of the failures of the service provider. Sometimes the customer gets it wrong and blames you unfairly. You still need to handle it though.

Customers also expect there to be a row as that is what their past experiences have taught them. Empathy at this early stage is critical. When you empathise you effectively show great understanding and put yourself in their shoes. They don't want your sympathy but they do want your empathy. Phrases such as '*You must be really disappointed about that*' or '*I'm sorry that you've had a bad experience*' will usually help to calm them down. They will appreciate your level of understanding for their predicament. Don't worry, when you empathise, you're not agreeing with their issue. You're simply showing that you're listening.

If you are defensive or argumentative, that will inflate the situation. More than likely the eventual solution will then cost you money in compensation of some sort.

P – Probe

Customers will have told you their stories in their own words and in their own ways. The stories may have been peppered with jargon or profanities, or with limited or useless information which is not always helpful to you. In order to understand the real issue, the implications and indeed, the causes of the problem, you will need to establish the full facts. That is why you must ask appropriate questions to get the detail.

Ask questions to get clarity, such as '*what exactly happened?*' or '*what time were you actually expecting it?*' Open-ended questions will get much more information in a nice soft way than closed-ended questions (such as '*did you order it yourself?*' or '*did you expect it at 3 pm?*').

C – Clarify your understanding of the situation

Having heard the customer's point, summarise your full understanding of the situation and what happened. This has the effect of showing the customer that you have listened fully and that you care. It also gives you the opportunity to check if you've missed an important piece of information. It acts as a bridge between the complaint and the next steps and sends a gentle message to the customer that you are now about to move on to finding a solution.

A – Agree an action

Having effectively summarised your understanding of the customer's complaint, it is now time to agree a solution. *Agreeing* on a solution is usually the better tactic here than *telling* the customer what you will do. By *telling*, you might risk disagreement which you may have to back down from again. Usually customers will be reasonable at this point, particularly if they feel you have listened, empathised and truly apologised for their inconvenience. Ask: '*What would you like me to do about it for you?*'

F – Follow-up

Having secured agreement on an appropriate solution and course of action, don't screw it up by not following through on your promises. Cynical customers of course expect you to forget and mess up again. Prove them wrong and show that you truly have taken their complaints seriously.

Solution matrix

As mentioned earlier, not all complaints are that big a deal or are even caused by you or your company. Nevertheless, if a customer has complained, you have a duty to do something about it. In doing something there are two considerations:

- How big is the effect of the issue that went wrong?
- Who is responsible?

Having listened and then summarised your understanding, plot the issue into one of the four quadrants and act accordingly.

High Impact on Customer	**Be a Hero and Help**	**Give the Red Carpet Treatment**
Low Impact on Customer	**Empathise**	**Empathise and Fix**
	We're not responsible or It wasn't caused by us	We caused it and We're responsible

Low impact/We didn't cause it

An example of this is where customers might complain about the weather as they embark on their bus tour. You certainly didn't cause it, but you can make the customers feel that you're disappointed for them.

High impact/We didn't cause it

If customers have been let down by, say their own driver, you might like to take the opportunity to be a 'hero' and find a solution really quickly.

Low impact/We did cause it

Imagine a situation where a customer was disappointed to find that a replacement lid for a Fissler cookpot hadn't arrived in store as promised. Think of the inconvenience involved. You and your supplier have caused the problem and it is incumbent on you to take responsibility and urgently fix the problem.

High impact/We did cause it

Imagine if a customer was hurt by slipping on the wet floor of your reception area. The business has caused that and it could be serious. You should do everything in your power to show that you care and are taking responsibility. Perhaps arrange for a taxi home, a bouquet of flowers or more if needed.

Complaints management and recording

It is good practice to record all complaints. It sends a message to the whole organisation that this is negatively affecting the brand. The other purpose of recording complaints is to use them as key performance indicators (KPIs) for departments and individuals.

Use this data to ensure that corrective action is taken to reduce, mitigate or eliminate repeats of the same issue in the future.

> *We are tired out in making complaints and getting no redress.*
> Joseph Brant, Mohawk and Political Military Leader, 1743–1807

When recording complaints, many organisations also classify them under the 4 Ps of Product, People, Place and Process, and that helps for trend reporting. The data will then give you, the leader, evidence when feeding back to your own teams, manufacturers, partners or suppliers.

SUMMARY

Complaints are a reality for most companies. Despite your best efforts to get it right the first time, every time, operational things do go wrong. It may be a batch issue, human error, or third party service slip-up. The point is that if and when complaints do occur, your company culture should see them as an opportunity to recover and prevent customer disappointment.

Research shows us that only 4% of customers actually complain (usually more when the ticket value is higher). Of the 96% that don't complain, 91% of them defect from you. These are scary numbers and show the importance of having a culture of service recovery.

Key Takeaways:

- Complaints from customers give you a second chance to *get it right the first time* – so don't mess up
- Complaints properly handled save you money in the long run
- Train your people on the EPCAF model
  - *Empathise*
  - *Probe for more detail*
  - *Confirm your understanding of the issue*
  - *Agree an action*
  - *Follow-up*

Key Questions For You:

- Is service recovery embedded in your culture, or is it more the norm to see complaining customers as a pain in the neck?
- Do your suppliers and partners know how seriously you take complaints and that you record them?

Watch For These Pitfalls:

- There is often cynicism and ambivalence about complaints; don't let that creep into your organisation
- Complaints tend to escalate quite quickly and the cost of recovery often goes up with that escalation

Chapter Eleven

Measure and Take Corrective Action

Picture yourself on a very hot day in a room in your office. The sun is splitting the stones outside and creating shadows all over the street. The pedestrians are wearing very light clothing and are in good spirits with their sunglasses on. There is a humming noise in the background that you don't even hear as you're busy listening to a presentation from your colleague. As the meeting progresses the room gets warmer, so you stand up and check the air-conditioning unit on the wall. You notice that the thermostat is set to 24 so you lower it. After a few minutes the room temperature cools to a more acceptable level and you get comfortable again.

For this story to have meaning, think of the thermostat in the air-conditioning unit. That is what gives you accurate information about the real temperature in the room. You yourself knew there was something not quite right, and that in itself has value. However, to know exactly what corrective action to take required an accurate thermostat.

Professional sports players review video clips of their last game, competition or fight to see where they did well, where they made mistakes and how they might improve. That feedback is essential to help them in preparation for their next game.

Organisations that are serious about giving consistently great service also value the importance of measuring what customers think of them. For sure, most organisations know instinctively if they are giving good or bad service. Some organisations even measure the success of their service by the number of complaints that they get. *'But we're not getting many complaints!'* Think about that for a minute. Doesn't it sound very negative?

If the number of complaints are reducing, that of course is a good measure. But if that is the only measure, be careful. That assumes that every customer that has a bad experience actually tells you. Of course, we know from an earlier chapter that they don't. Monitoring complaints is a good thing to do, as you will read in the chapter on service recovery, but it's not enough.

As with a thermostat, having a way of measuring what your customers think of you enables you to take corrective action accordingly. The difference is that a thermostat measures one thing only: the temperature. A well designed structured feedback survey should give you much more than a single piece of information. It should tell you what parts of your customers' experience need to improve and which are satisfactory.

Remember too that measurement is only part of the job. Taking corrective action to act on the feedback and improve on any shortcomings is the critical piece.

Feedback tools

The main options on how to receive customer feedback include:

1. Mystery shopping
2. Observation
3. One-to-ones and focus groups
4. Suggestion box
5. Surveys

1. Mystery shopping

Mystery shopping as a concept has been around for some time. Typically the organisation engages an external service provider of mystery shopping. Between the two parties, they'll agree a set of questions that reflect the interaction with the customer and *what good looks like*. This might be the process of a sale with a sales assistant, the check-in at a hotel, the service in a restaurant, the telephone call to a contact centre, the navigation through an on-line purchase or the delivery by a driver. All touchpoints for the customer should be considered.

The external agency usually has a panel of 'customers', contractors or 'professional shoppers' who are then requested to carry out an agreed number of shops (or interactions) with your business. The 'mystery shoppers' will act as if they were real customers and then make judgements on how they were treated against a pre-determined checklist. The scores are then collated and presented back to the client.

This is intended to be an objective measurement process. After all, customers should get a consistent experience appropriate to the brand, every single time. The purpose of mystery shopping is to spot-check that at varying times. It does have a number of potential risks as follows:

- The 'mystery shopper' might possibly approach the shopping experience in quite a mechanical way, lacking the real emotion that a true shopper would attach to the same experience.

- To build a fair reflection of the quality of the service, there should preferably be five shops completed per location within whatever time frame you'll be reporting on, so as to achieve an average and consistent rating.
- Mystery shoppers tend to behave differently to real shoppers. That alerts clever sales assistants to spot them fairly quickly and turn on the charm immediately just for that encounter. That potentially undermines the process and does not reflect accurately on the overall experience for all customers.

If you choose to engage a mystery shopping service, have a conversation with your provider in advance so as to mitigate these risks.

2. *Observation*

Once the service has been defined, agreed upon, and communicated to all, managers might take time out every now and then to simply observe how front line personnel are speaking to and treating customers. Check for tone of voice, courtesy, accuracy, helpfulness, words used, attitude, process and more. After observing, managers should then follow up with that colleague and give them feedback, regardless of whether it is good or bad. The value of instant feedback is that there is no possibility of memory loss or dilution of message due to time delay.

3. *One-to-ones and focus groups*

You'll have been in a restaurant many times in your life where the waiter has asked, '*Is everything all right with your meal?*' On the one hand, it is good that they care. On the other hand, it is too often done with no meaning or real intent to establish your view. Even the question is a closed question, and not likely to get more than a 'yes or no' answer. That may vary across cultures but in the main, diners usually respond simply with 'yes, thanks'.

Making proactive contact with a customer and asking, '*How do you feel about our service today?*' or '*How could we improve our service for you?*' is so much more powerful. These are open questions that will get comments other than 'Yes' or 'No'. Direct and immediate feedback is incredibly valuable if done correctly and with authenticity. Customers will immediately recognise you genuinely want to know how they feel and will give you feedback that is like gold dust to your business.

Focus groups will do the same thing. But be careful: if they are not safely facilitated they can become very negative. Pick candidates that are individual in thought and who will not just go along with others because they don't want to upset, disagree or offend. The focus group should be short, sharp and structured.

Set the scene initially by outlining your brand positioning. If you don't do that, the focus group members won't have context. For example, you may proudly be a three star brand, but if the focus group members give you feedback against the backdrop of five star, that will undermine the process.

4. Suggestion box

Suggestion boxes, or cards left on the dining table or reception desk, are good for getting quick and short comments. They typically ask a short few questions about the experience. They are positive in that they capture the immediate emotions of the customer. And emotions influence the customer's willingness to return or not.

The mix of questions vary and there is no universal pattern to them. But there is one question that will have the most value to you! *'Mr/Ms Customer, thank you for shopping/dining/staying with us today. We try hard to give you the best experience we can. What is the one thing we could improve on in the future?'* That will focus customers and they will more than likely give you a valuable verbatim comment.

5. Surveys

Surveys are a structured way of getting customers' written/typed views on their experiences, using a set of questions that mirrors their experience at key touchpoints. For B2C organisations, that will include the whole shopping/dining experience. For B2Bs, that should include all touchpoints from the time of ordering all the way through to deliveries.

Surveys are a powerful way of identifying strengths and weaknesses in your proposition and will help you to improve.

How to conduct great surveys

A professional survey should be seen to be independent. If customers suspect that they can be identified in the survey that they are being asked to complete, they may not be as honest as they could be. That of course is not true in every case, but just to be sure, you might be better off using an external agency.

Pick your agency carefully. There are many providers that focus mainly on the technology and the mechanics of how to get the feedback as if that was all that mattered. There is much more to it than that. What is more important is asking the right questions in the first place. Making sense of the feedback is of even more importance.

There are three elements that make up a well-run customer survey:

1. Set the questions
2. Gather the feedback
3. Present the results

1. Set the questions

You have lots of choices here about the style of survey that you want to do. There are lots of conceptual questions you can ask that will measure customer satisfaction, such as, *'How satisfied were you with the service today?'* These are important questions but are not enough on their own. What can you do with the result, regardless of whether you score 10% or 90%? It is much more important to know what elements of the service the customer is satisfied or dissatisfied with, so that you can act on the feedback.

For example, there is a technological solution often seen in airports and stores. It is a panel with four buttons, ranging from green (very satisfied) to red (very dissatisfied). After going through security in Heathrow Airport, you can press one of the four buttons on this machine. Each button represents your level of satisfaction with the security screening in particular. A percentage of travellers do of course press a button, which gets aggregated to a cumulative score. That is very helpful to the airport operator as they get specific feedback on that element of the customer journey, but they don't know why travellers feel the way they do. If they get a poor score, how do they know what to fix? Is it due to the long queue, or the behaviour of staff? What about the availability of seating to put shoes back on?

Once again, it's important to acknowledge the positive in this methodology. It means that customer experience is on the agenda of management and they are measuring it. They can also measure satisfaction at various stages of the journey. The piece that is missing is understanding the specifics. After all, the purpose of conducting surveys is ultimately to improve things.

There are other questions that are known as 'driver' questions. This is where you break down all the touchpoints in the customer journey and then ask questions at a more granular level to determine the cause and effect.

If you are B2B, draw up the full process from the point customers place an order with you, through to when they make payment. Here are the categories in a recent B2B beverage distributor:

- Order process on-line
- Order process on the telephone
- Order process with sales representative
- Pack sizes
- Pallet sizes
- Delivery schedule
- Delivery driver
- Paperwork
- Payment process
- Returns process

Here are some sample points to check:

- I am informed of out-of-stocks at time of ordering
- Placing orders directly with xxx is efficient
- Team members are courteous
- Deliveries arrive as promised
- Deliveries are complete
- Out-of-stocks are communicated in good time
- Goods arrive in good condition
- Truck crews are well presented
- I know who to contact each time I have a problem
- Problems are followed-through quickly

- I am informed of promotions in good time
- Promotions happen often enough
- Pricing of products is sufficiently competitive

Each category will have its own set of questions relevant to your process. Ensure your questions are clear and concise. Avoid double-barrel questions where the respondent is unsure which part of the question is most important. For example, avoid these questions:

- The delivery arrived on-time and in full
- The truck crews are professional and courteous
- The sales representative was knowledgeable and helpful

If you are a retailer, you will also want feedback on all touchpoints. Remember the 3-legged stool from earlier. You need to ask relevant questions in each category under *Product*, *People* and *Place*.

Keep the questionnaire to a reasonable length. Under ten minutes is safe as anything longer will encourage opt-outs before customers get to the end.

You also have choices about the rating scale that you use. For speed, the machine mentioned above has only four options. There is no middle ground, where respondents might opt for the middle one. By only allowing four buttons, customers will immediately have to decide if they are happy or not. If they press either of the lower two, we'll know they're unhappy, and so on. A four-button survey indicates direction of feeling, rather than the intensity.

Longer surveys tend to use a scale of either 1–5, 1–7 or 1–10. The 1–10 option will detect the level of intensity of feeling and is more the norm for longer surveys. Respondents usually take a bit longer to consider their responses. But there is always a balance to be struck. There are lots of academic points of view to support all options. The best thing is to try them out and test what works best for you.

You might also consider including some opportunities for verbatim comments. Perhaps at the end of each group of questions, you ask what is known as a qualitative question (quantitative questions have a scoring option, qualitative questions have a narrative option only). By seeking open-ended verbatim comments, you may get rich comments and feelings. Here is a very powerful verbatim question: '*What is the <u>one</u> thing that would make you feel better about...?*'

2. *Gather the feedback*

The most common way to gather insights is on-line. There are a number of companies that will provide a platform for you to gather feedback through their portals. CFIGroup.com is one such company. All questions present themselves for scoring and the averaging is going on in the background.

You can also do it yourself by using an on-line tool such as SurveyMonkey. With this, you can carry out your own survey at no cost. However, be careful. The value in using external expertise is not for the platform or portal. The value is in the support you get in designing the questions in the first place and then making sense of the feedback.

You also need to consider who to invite to participate. Do you ask all customers, or segment them so you can get their feedback on a recent experience? Do you ask non-customers so that you can establish why they didn't buy from you?

Selfridges in UK had a programme going for a few years where they used an external provider who had a panel of 'paid customers' to shop in the store or on-line. Those customers had to actually buy something from Selfridges and they got a cheque for doing so. That was the incentive and it worked. Each month, Selfridges got feedback from the service provider of what the panel of customers thought. Of course there were flaws in this, as some of the panel were doing this just for the money and would often return the purchase for a refund later. Nevertheless, the programme did produce trend reports and that's what matters.

In a later iteration of the same programme, Selfridges stopped using 'paid customers'. Instead they switched to a provider that used *actual* customers. These customers were discovered by inserting a printed invite on each till receipt, encouraging customers to log on and give feedback. There was an incentive to get the number of respondents up, which was done by telling customers that they'd be in with a chance to win a £1000 Selfridges gift voucher. The incentive did make a difference and they got enough respondents in each department to give a score each month.

For the on-line survey, they added a few lines of code so that for every fourth visitor to the site, a pop-up window would appear inviting the visitor to participate in the survey. The percentage of respondents on-line and indeed in store was very low. But it is a numbers game and so long as they had at least five shoppers per department per month, the results were deemed to be statistically valid. If the number of responses was less than five, those responses were simply ignored and dumped.

3. Present the results

Most likely the technology that you use will accommodate reports through slicing and dicing the results across locations, departments and any other demographics you might include in the survey. But numbers and graphs alone are just data. The insights that you extract from the numbers are much more important. Here are some thoughts to inspire you to interrogate the numbers:

- What are the highs and lows?
- What is the cause of these variances?
- How do these scores compare to your competition (if you can find out)?
- Is there a link between some of the categories of questions?
- Which categories of questions came out highest or lowest?
- Do the highs and lows correlate to a particular leader or department head?
- Do the highs and lows correlate to a particular route to market?

- How are the numbers trending between this survey and previous surveys? (The core scores that you achieve are much less important than the trend over time.)

Net Promoter Score (NPS)

Net Promoter Score (NPS) is a new way of measuring customer loyalty developed by (and a registered trademark of) Fred Reichheld, Bain & Company, and Satmetrix. NPS has been widely adopted by large and small corporations around the globe.

NPS is calculated based on responses to a single question: '*How likely is it that you would recommend xxxx product/service to a friend or colleague?*' The scoring options range between 0–10. Of all questions in a survey, this question is considered to be the single most important question, as customers are more likely or less likely to recommend their experiences to others.

Those who respond with a score of 9 to 10 are called *Promoters* and are considered likely to buy more. It is thought that they will remain as customers for longer, and make positive referrals to other potential customers. Those who respond with a score of 0 to 6 are deemed to be *Detractors*. They are less likely to return in the future or to recommend the service provider to others. Responses of 7 and 8 are considered *Passives*, sitting between Promoters and Detractors. The Net Promoter Score is calculated by subtracting the percentage of customers who are Detractors from the percentage of customers who are Promoters. Those who scored 7 or 8 are simply ignored.

NPS can be as low as −100 (where everyone is a detractor) or as high as +100 (where everyone is a promoter). An NPS that is positive (higher than zero) is good, and an NPS of +50 is excellent. For purposes of calculating a Net Promoter Score, the number of Passives are included in the overall number of respondents. That decreases the percentage of detractors and promoters.

The NPS score gives you a sense of how customers are feeling after their interactions. It doesn't give you the reason why, so other questions are of course critical to establish the reasons. Additional questions should be included to better understand the reasons why and the perception of various products and services. These additional questions help a company rate the relative importance of these other parts of the business in the overall score.

There are some potential and controversial downsides to using NPS. One is to do with international differences. For example, respondents in the Netherlands don't tend to give high scores in surveys. It seems to be a cultural thing where even when they are extremely satisfied, they are only likely to give 7s and 8s. In some other countries, perhaps the US or the Philippines, people are more willing and generous with their scoring. Many international businesses with global offices would feel this is a flaw. Another issue is that all respondents that give a score between 0–6 are grouped in the same category. Is it fair to say that a customer giving a score of 6 feels quite as annoyed as one giving 0? Yet they are grouped together.

Certainly in recent times, banks and others are re-designing their complete customer surveys and hanging them out of the NPS methodology. As a concept it is gaining traction and has the added value of motivating organisations to not be laggards or to become best in their industries. Another great thing about an NPS score is that it allows your organisation to compare itself to other larger or smaller companies, across all industries. It satisfies board members who for years have been looking for one simple customer feedback metric.

Post-feedback corrective actions

To re-iterate a point made earlier in this chapter, having a way of measuring what your customers think of you enables you to take corrective action accordingly. If you don't take action, what's the point in measuring in the first place?

Note however that reactions to feedback can vary significantly among different people. Here is a typical flow of how reactions can evolve. Of course you may not know in advance how any individual will react, so be respectful in your delivery of the results. Prepare your message by acknowledging this flow.

An initial immediate reaction might be *shock*, *anger* or *denial*. If the recipient of the feedback gets stuck on any of these three, you're unlikely to get agreement on corrective actions. People might be shocked if this is the first time they're receiving this type of feedback, or if there has been a significant change since the previous survey. Anger is another possibility, which might be visible (negative facial expressions or raised voice). Denial is where the recipient challenges the integrity of the survey itself and is using that approach as a defence mechanism to dispute the results.

You'll need to help the recipients *understand* the feedback. Perhaps explain the mechanics, the logic, the process, or the questions. Reassure them that the feedback may be perception, not actual reality. This latter comment often allows recipients of feedback to let go of their defences and move on.

After *understanding* the next phase is *acceptance*. It's fair to say that some people will accept the feedback immediately without defence or question. For others, you will need to bring them on the journey by helping them to understand it.

The final phase is *action*, which is the whole point of the exercise.

In the Selfridges programme, the results were fed back to each department manager and store manager on a monthly basis. They were expected to put plans in place to take corrective action on those elements that scored the lowest. To do that, they were encouraged to do root cause analysis of the problem, rather than just short term fixes.

At a macro level, if you are seeing a pattern of low scores across the board, those issues need to be addressed centrally. Root cause analysis is about asking '*Why?*' and '*So what?*' several times. When you ask it the first time and get an initial answer, ask the '*Why?*' and '*So what?*' questions again about that answer. Continue that drilling down till you get to the root cause. Here is an example:

- The survey feedback illustrated an issue with lack of knowledge by the sales team. *Why?*

- A new range of product arrived recently.
  So what?
- The range was not introduced to the team and they were not trained.
  Why not?
- The supplier was due to do it but didn't turn up.
  Etc.

To be serious about taking corrective action that has long term effect, you will need to identify causes and obstacles. Otherwise, you may get a short term uplift but then fall back to lower scores again very soon.

Remember too that people that are nearest to a problem are often nearest to the solution. Engage the relevant team in the process of problem resolution and corrective actions.

For the most part, customer experience is delivered by people. How you handle feedback with people on the front line is critical. They need to know that you are getting feedback. They also need to know that there will be consequences for repeat offenders. You may agree that everyone is permitted one chance to get it wrong, just like the 'yellow card' in football. However, for a second offence in football, the player gets a red card and is sent off. That punishment might sound a bit extreme but you have to decide what is appropriate for your organisation. If the 'offence' was committed due to circumstances outside the team member's control, perhaps no discipline is appropriate. If it was entirely the team member's fault, you have hard decisions to make.

Clearly in a modern day work environment, you'd much rather have a positive reinforcement management style. When scores are good, make sure to let the team or person know.

SUMMARY

It is critical that you measure what your customers think of you and the level of customer experience your organisation gives. There are a number of effective ways to gather that feedback that all have value. You need to pick the one that is right for you, your customers and your budget.

Net Promoter Score (NPS) is a new way of measuring customer satisfaction that is linked to just one question: '*How likely is it that you would recommend xxxx product/service to a friend or colleague?*' It has lots of positives in that it allows comparisons within and across industries and around the globe. Be careful however as there are lots of negative reactions to NPS. You just need to pick a measurement approach that is right for you.

Key Takeaways:

- Whichever feedback methodology you select, test it a few times
- Surveys professionally administered are a powerful way of getting quality and objective feedback
- Regardless of how you gather the feedback, take time to identify the right questions first
- The actual scores that you get are not as important as the trends over time in resurveys

Key Questions For You:

- If feedback scores (such as NPS) are being discussed at your board meetings, that is a good thing, but are you also exploring the causes of those scores?
- Are corrective actions an agenda item?

Watch For These Pitfalls:

- If all your focus goes into the mechanics of a survey (gathering the data) rather than taking time to getting the questions right, it'll be a futile exercise
- Feedback results should always be followed by considered root-cause analysis and lead to corrective actions

PART FOUR

HOW TO PUT IT ALL TO WORK FOR YOU

TAKE INSPIRATION FROM SELFRIDGES

Note from the author

As you reflect on the various ideas presented here, take comfort from knowing that they have all been tried and tested in various organisations across industry over the years. Some elements may be more appropriate than others and that's up to you. However, you'll find it very hard to argue with the reality that excellence in customer experience is, without doubt, the new battleground for all businesses in all industries. Not only that, as the world continues to change due to sociological, technological, economical and political drivers, you will also find that the level of customer services gets higher and higher. Customer expectations keep increasing on the back of all that. Premium is the new black!

Your challenge now is to find a way to introduce the concept to your organisation and to keep it going for the long term as part of your new business model. Regardless of your size, you can take some inspiration from how Selfridges did it.

After the business was purchased by its current owner, I was invited to support the significant change agenda that followed. From 2004 to 2013, I was heavily involved in facilitating and supporting the change agenda, which included setting a new North Star for the business and shaping a new culture that paid respect to the founder's heritage and the family values of its new owner.

In the examples that follow you will get a sense of the task that was undertaken. If the ultimate measure of success for a commercial business is measured in financial terms, this transformation has been a tremendous success. If the measure is less about financial metrics but more about people, customers, awards, innovation, culture, regard from peers and media commentary, then the Selfridges story is still a success. You of course will form your own view.

Alan O'Neill

Selfridges UK

Selfridges Department Store is a British institution. Founded by Gordon Selfridge in 1909, it has become an icon for innovation, creativity and world class retailing. With a flagship store in London, two in Manchester, one in Birmingham and an on-line store – the Oxford Street store wasn't always one of the most profitable stores in the world. That recent success can be attributed to its new owners and management team.

Galen and Hillary Weston, their daughter Alannah (ex-Creative Director of Selfridges UK) and Paul Kelly (Managing Director since 2004) are experienced retailers with a passion for giving world class customer experience. The family acquired the business in 2004 and subsequently merged it into the worldwide Selfridges Group. Alannah Weston is the Deputy Chairman and Paul Kelly is now the Managing Director of the Group. The other stores in the global Selfridges Group include Holt Renfrew in Canada, Brown Thomas in Ireland, deBijenkorf in the Netherlands and more recently Arnotts in Dublin. They all have reputations in their respective markets for great customer experience.

When the family bought Selfridges, they inherited an organisation with a great heritage and brand equity. But there was much more financial potential than what was being achieved prior to purchase. With a relentless focus on detail, the profits grew by 180% in the initial six years after the takeover. It's no coincidence that the customer satisfaction scores moved up 18 points in the same period. This illustrates that there is an intrinsic link between great service and higher sales.

After winning the award in 2010 for *Best Department Store of the Year* (as voted by the Global Department Store Summit), again in 2012, and twice more since then, Selfridges have a lot to shout about. One of the criteria for this global award is excellence in customer experience. Selfridges are known for their great people, fantastic product range and an energy that now seems to be a living organism that you can almost touch in store. Selfridges UK is now led by current Managing Director Anne Pitcher.

In the UK business, customer service scores were not always so high. There was a period of time where customer experience levels slipped at the expense of focusing on other factors. Perhaps in the latter part of the 1990s, there were other views on what great customer experience should be. In recent times, there has been a return to ensuring the basics of great customer experience are to the fore. This is also a weekly boardroom agenda item, unlike other organisations, where customer experience is often delegated down the line to an operational level only.

Selfridges will acknowledge even today that there is more work to be done in taking service to the next level. It's a cliché, but great retailing is all about the detail. There is no room for relaxing on any element of the retail mix, which is made up of people, product, service, environment and profitability.

In the following pages are some of the steps that Selfridges took to excel in customer experience. You'll recognise all of them from the detail shown in this book. They include:

1. Vision, strategy and culture that puts customer experience high on the agenda
2. *What good looks like*

3. Training and Communications
4. Obstacles
5. Incentives and consequences
6. Managers as role models
7. Monitor and give feedback
8. Measure progress
9. Service recovery

1. Vision, Strategy and Culture

After settling in and getting to grips with the new business, the board took time out to refresh the North Star for the business. The process of designing a new vision and mission involved a process of consultation with key stakeholders, trawling through archives back to when the business was founded and getting clarity on the DNA of the brand. For example, while the store has a very strong luxury feel to it, the heritage is all about inclusivity rather than exclusivity. When Gordon opened the store in 1909 he sent out an invitation to the public saying that 'everyone is welcome'.

Luxury would almost suggest a level of exclusivity. Instead Selfridges agreed a new vision and mission as follows:

- *Vision*: To be the destination for extraordinary experiences
- *Mission*: We are here to surprise, amaze and amuse our customers – and everyone is welcome

The process for developing your North Star culminates with a wordsmithing job. The words chosen by Selfridges were very considered and were not just the result of a two-minute conversation around the table! It took a number of weeks of consideration and involvement by key stakeholders. For clarity, the vision statement is where you aspire to be as a brand. You're not there yet, otherwise it wouldn't be a vision and would certainly not be motivational or aspirational. Think of the vision as: *'What do you want to be when you grow up?'*

The mission statement is more about why you exist. Think of that like Tom Cruise in the *Mission Impossible* films: *'Your mission, if you choose to accept it, is...'*

Your vision and mission statements should satisfy these questions:

- How do we currently rate ourselves in line with those words?
- What assumptions are we making?
- How big do we want to be?
- What are we famous for?
- Why should anyone care?
- How do people feel about being part of it?
- What does each stakeholder think or care?
- Is it inspirational and can we be passionate about it?

Strategy

There was a time when large organisations would develop a five year plan. That was about having a big picture road map that guided the business on where it was going for the next five years. But as the world has become much more fast-changing and fluid, five year plans are less the norm. The alternative is to have a two year or three year rolling strategy. Selfridges developed a five year plan but allowed themselves the time to refresh it each subsequent year.

In the process of shaping the refreshed strategy, the customer was at the centre of their thinking. Lots of consideration was given to how the marketplace was changing, how customers are changing and indeed how employees are changing. A key metric in the new plan was the customer survey feedback as described in an earlier chapter.

Culture

You will have seen from an earlier chapter the importance of culture in delivering on an organisation's ambition and strategy. The main tool used in Selfridges was 'values'. Through a comprehensive process of discovery and design, a new set of values were formed that would shape the business for the future. You will not be surprised to see the first value here referring to the 'customer'.

- Think customer
- Show and earn respect
- Know your stuff
- Be pacey and positive
- Own it and deliver

The values were brought to life in many tactical ways. Indicative behaviours for each value were outlined. Then the values were included in all internal communications, in objective setting for executives and middle managers, in recruitment and training, in annual nominations and awards, and in internal surveys.

The trap many organisations fall into is that they develop a set of values and then do nothing with them. That is such a missed opportunity, as values shaped the extraordinary success that Selfridges have enjoyed since 2004.

2. What good looks like

The mix of product in the Selfridges business is incredibly vast. They are famous for having top global designer brands, such as Chanel, in close proximity to high-street high-fashion brands like Primark, all under one roof and on the same floor. This fits with their brand DNA and ambition to be inclusive. Nevertheless, *what good looks like* in terms of customer experience will of course differ across the departments. The customer spending £20 on a top will certainly get a premium experience, in terms of the department layout and assistance from the salesperson. But the customer in Chanel spending

£2,000 will get a different level of experience. More time will obviously be taken with the customers, the ambience will be much more upscale and the fitting rooms will be more spacious.

In such a large, diverse and eclectic mix across all six floors in London (and the regional stores), *what good looks like* was defined. Using the 3-legged stool described earlier (*product, people and place*), the teams from each department were engaged in a series of training and communications workshops to give their input. That was a significant piece of work that paid dividends in a number of ways. Agreement on standards was reached across the departments. By engaging the teams in the process, they felt more engaged and empowered. The detail was used to feed into the customer feedback surveys (more later).

All of this was documented and is regularly reviewed and updated.

3. Training and Communications

Training

Every sales associate was trained on the Selfridges selling ceremony, or the eight steps shown in the earlier chapter on People. The selling ceremony merged with how to best deliver a great customer experience on the shop floor. It was called the selling ceremony because no business should be afraid to recognise that sales are the engine of the business. Customers do want to be sold to but they also want to be treated with a level of authenticity and respect. Associates were trained on how to best *connect* with customers, how to *consult* with them on their needs and how to professionally *conclude* the interaction.

Managers were trained on how to give inspirational briefings and the values also played a big part in that. In every department in every store, the sales associates are rostered to be in the store at least fifteen minutes before the doors open. In that time, every single one of them attends a briefing session where customer experience (using the 3-legged stool framework) is re-iterated.

When new recruits join the business, they go through an induction programme where they learn about the heritage, the brand, where customer experience fits in, the values and how much emphasis is placed on them.

Values launch

When the new values were initially launched, there was a very comprehensive communications cascade from the senior management team. Values workshops were conducted throughout the whole organisation, using a full suite of collateral (posters, slide decks, newsletters, screen savers, mouse mats, notebooks, pens, etc.) Every department in head office, on the shop floors and in back offices participated in a workshop localised to their department, where they discussed the context in which the values sat. They also discussed what the values meant to them and how they as a department could bring them to life. Although there was a pre-defined set of indicative behaviours agreed at head-office level for each value, each department then expanded on those with other behaviours relevant to their own department.

Objectives

In terms of communications, there is another initiative that is having a big effect on managers. There is an objectives process, where every director and manager is given three objectives to deliver on per year. An objective is a project or task that will take the business to another level. Objectives are not just day-job tasks; they are intended to reflect a quantum leap for the business. Some examples might include launching a new department, migrating from an old IT system to a new one, negotiating a new supply-chain partner or delivering a new recruitment process.

However, one of the objectives was always set aside to be a 'personal objective'. A personal objective is something that individuals have to improve about their own management style. The values and indicative behaviours were the framework within which the personal objective would be drawn from. Samples for a new recruit might include embracing the Selfridges culture. For existing managers, samples might include proactively supporting colleagues in areas outside one's immediate remit, being more trusting with one's peers or being more accountable.

The objectives were taken very seriously, so much so that they were included in annual performance and development plans. The achievement of all objectives, including personal ones, also had an effect on bonuses.

Newsletter

An internal newsletter was published weekly where key messages were communicated to all. This also included positive stories and examples of how the values were being lived, customer survey feedback scores, and of course all the other business stuff such as new brands and general business performance.

Awards ceremony

Selfridges hold an annual awards ceremony where people who are nominated during the year are invited to an 'Oscars Night' type ceremony. There are several nomination categories including one for each value, best salesperson, best leader and best at customer service. The nominations are submitted by peers and managers throughout the year and there is a very fair and objective weighting process for deciding on the winners.

4. *Obstacles*

Despite the best efforts of any business to deliver excellent service every day, the reality of life is that obstacles will emerge. They might be practical resource or operational issues, or systems or processes. This came to light in a workshop for a team on the cheese counter.

On one occasion, customer survey results were lower than standard for the department. As this was unacceptable, the full team had to participate in a workshop to hear again about the importance of customer service. During the workshop the team identified and debated some obstacles that they were experiencing regularly. One issue was that tourist customers were complaining that they wanted to bring the British cheese that they were buying back to their own countries. But Selfridges did not offer a vacuum-pack service. This was causing disgruntlement and costing sales.

It would have so easy to railroad the customer service message once again and not listen, but that would have cost the business dearly. Instead the team were listened to and a vacuum-pack machine was purchased for very little money. Because of that (and some other issues) customer service scores and sales increased. The morale in the team also improved because they had been listened to and respected.

That doesn't mean that every obstacle identified by the team can or should be acted upon. However, you do have to at least listen. If there are some issues raised that are either outside the team's control or just plain ridiculous, of course you have to manage expectations and push back.

5. Incentives and consequences

In an ideal world, you might expect that everybody should give excellent service every single time. Of course many do, but salespeople also respond well when incentives and consequences are in place. Selfridges developed an incentive programme linked to the customer survey programme. When individual team members got individual scores of 100%, they got the opportunity to win cash prizes. This was effective, as the winners were publicly recognised and it became an incentive for others.

Likewise, there were consequences in place for poor scores. Selfridges are certainly not a vindictive organisation. However, if team members were identified as giving poor service through the survey mechanism or manager observation, they were pulled up on it. Repeat offenders were encouraged to find their magic in another organisation. After all, one bad apple can have an effect across the board, with the customers they come in contact with and indeed with their colleagues. This was done with proper procedures and the reasons were made very clear.

Far too many organisations do not deal with this effectively. They tend to move people around rather than face up to the difficult task of giving discipline. If a standard has been set that reflects the brand DNA, everybody has a duty to live up to that every single day. There are much bigger stakes at play here that should not be allowed to be jeopardised by a repeat offender.

6. Managers as role models

Managers are beacons for their own departments. You'll have heard the expression '*Monkeys see, monkeys do*'. While that is in no way meant to offend anyone, it's just an analogy for one of life's realities. Another example is with a parent and child. A child learns from what they see their parents doing and saying. Managers in Selfridges are expected to recognise that they as individuals set the tone in their own departments. They are all expected to be role models and to lead by example.

That starts with their own appearances, how they greet customers, how they speak to their colleagues, how they behave in meetings, and more. It might also apply to how they speak about customers in their absence. If after dealing with a difficult customer, a manager speaks negatively about that customer, what message does that convey to the team? Does that become the norm for how customers are regarded?

The values are the framework and indicative behaviours are listed for each one. At the very least, managers should display those behaviours every day.

7. Monitor and give feedback

Managers should give priority to observing how their teams interact with customers. A head office manager whose team are not customer-facing may be interacting with suppliers or internal customers, i.e. other departments. If people are speaking in unacceptable tones or are not following through and taking responsibility for actions, they should be called out on it.

Similarly, managers on the shop-floor should monitor how sales associates are interacting with customers. This might seem like a bit over the top. Doesn't modern management theory suggest that people should be trusted and empowered to just get on with it?

That is completely true, once individuals have proven that they can be left alone. There is too much at stake in terms of risk to your brand, if you stand back completely. Obviously in the early days of a person's time in your organisation, you need to monitor closely and give feedback. If after time people have proven themselves to be consistently good, you can stand back and leave them to it.

This is how Selfridges managers were encouraged to work with their teams. When they did observe consistently good work, they were encouraged to recognise that and give the employees positive feedback. When they observed inappropriate behaviour of any sort, they were encouraged to deal with that immediately, rather than storing it up for the next performance review.

8. Measure progress

Selfridges have had a number of programmes over the years for measuring customer satisfaction and experience. Mystery shopping was in place before the Westons took over. It was recording very high scores but it was felt that it wasn't a true measure of customer experience in the new world, where higher standards were set.

A new programme was introduced where real customers were prompted by a message on the receipt to give feedback on-line. This turned out to be a very effective programme that had great traction internally. It was so valued that department managers would often go looking for their results literally on the date they were due. The results also fed into the incentive programme described above, so that also focused attention.

The fact that the scores were also discussed at board level is an indicator of how much value was put on the programme.

9. Service recovery

For such a large business, the volume of queries, returns and complaints is significant. (That doesn't mean that service levels were bad across all stores.) In a volume business, process is needed to handle complaints. Selfridges have a back office located in Leicester where a team of people handled all telephone calls and enquiries for the whole business. They were trained on how to handle a complaint, using the EPCAF method described in the earlier chapter on service recovery. There was a metric associated with this which became a key performance indicator (KPI) for each store.

With so much focus on customer experience and with a growing business, the metric was associated with a percentage of transactions. Using a volume number is less appropriate in a high growth business.

More importantly was what happened afterwards. Each month the complaints were categorised under various headings, such as *people, product, place* and *process*. That meant that trends were easy to spot. Relevant store managers were given the scores for their stores and were expected to put corrective actions in place and report back on progress.

SUMMARY

The fact that Selfridges have won the award for *Best Department Store in the World* comes as no surprise, given their focus on the detail of retail. Customer experience starts at the top in the organisation, meaning the family and the board. Consequently the leadership know that not only is this dear to the owners' hearts, but it's also good for business.

There are lots of programmes in place to keep it on top of the agenda. It is framed in the values, objectives for managers, ongoing communications, feedback surveys and relentless continuous improvement.

Selfridges have of course embraced digital and now have an omni-channel business where sales on-line are growing exponentially. Achieving excellence on-line is a different challenge and in many ways, it's a voyage of learning by discovery. You too need to focus on two key elements: the customer, and the willingness and ability to cope with change.

Key Takeaways:

- Retail is going through more disruptive change than most other industries
- Regardless of your industry or size, the lessons of the Selfridges transformation will apply to you too

Key Questions For You:

- Is customer experience on your radar?
- Do your vision and mission (North Star) need to be refreshed in light of the significant changes in your competitive environment?
- Does your culture support your ambition?
- Do you have a programme that puts customers at the heart of your decision-making?

Watch For These Pitfalls:

- Values are so effective in shaping culture, but if they are not being lived they are pointless
- If the leadership team are not on-side, the cascade will not work
- Transformation such as what Selfridges went through needs a planned and tailored programme
- If you don't monitor, measure and take corrective actions, the programme will lose momentum